How to Start and Run
Your Own
Business

No spit. More polish.

There's nothing wrong with the old-fashioned lick and stick stamp.

Except that it is old-fashioned.

And it does look rather untidy, especially when there are a lot of them on one envelope.

Postage printed by a Pitney Bowes meter, on the other hand, looks altogether neater and more businesslike – regardless of how much or how little postage goes on each individual package or envelope.

Because you always end up with just one clear, franked impression.

Plus, if you choose, an imprint of your name and slogan.

What's more, every Pitney Bowes postage meter is backed with the largest servicing network in the business.

Which not only says something about our efficiency.

It helps to advertise yours.

Pitney Bowes plc, FREEPOST, Harlow, Essex CM19 5YF. Tel: 0279 26731.

Pitney Bowes

World leader in mailing systems.

How to Start and Run Your Own Business

M. Mogano

Graham & Trotman

First published in 1980
Second edition published in 1982
Third edition published in 1982
Fourth edition published in 1983
Fifth edition published in 1985

Graham & Trotman Limited
Sterling House
66 Wilton Road
London SWV 1DE
UK

Graham & Trotman Inc.
13 Park Avenue
Gaithersburg
MD 20877
USA

© M. Mogano, 1980, 1982, 1983, 1985

British Library Cataloguing in Publication Data

Mogano, M.
  How to start and run your own business.—5th ed.
  1. Small business—Great Britain—Management
  I. Title
  658'.022'0941   HD62.7

  ISBN: 0-86010-559-8
  ISBN: 0-86010-577-6 Pbk

Typeset in Great Britain by Bookworm Typesetting, Salford
Printed and bound in Great Britain by Garden City Press, Letchworth, Hertfordshire.

Contents

Chapter 1 **MAKING A START** 1
Weighing up your present situation • Looking
on the bright side • Write it down • What
about YOU? • Summing yourself up • Taking
advice • Your bank manager • People in the
trade • Small Firms Information Service • Use
your library • Chambers of trade and commerce • Professional advice • Weighing it all
up • The money angles •

Chapter 2 **INVESTIGATING THE MARKET** 14
Introduction • Don't forget the competion •
Cost considerations • Seasonal influences •
The uncontrollables • After the sale • Finding
out more •

Chapter 3 **FINDING START-UP MONEY AND** 25
USING IT EFFECTIVELY
Introduction • How to cost your project •
Your own stake • How to raise finance •
Government Guaranteed Loan Scheme • Busi-
ness Expansion Scheme • Approaching your
bank manager • Types of security • Lending
values • Keep your bank manager in touch •
Cash projections • Costing • Keeping records
• Credit control • Budgets • Break-even
charts • Useful ratios • Taxation • Annual
accounts • Sources and uses of funds •

Chapter 4 **GETTING THE BUSINESS GOING** 54
Finding premises • Communications • Plant
and machinery • Personnel • Stock •
Accounting methods • Buying an established
business • Franchise operations •

Chapter 5   TAKING PROFESSIONAL ADVICE   68
                 Introduction ● The 'right' status ● Four just
                 men ● Keep on the right side of the law ●
                 Some relevant Acts ● Insurance — what to
                 cover ● You and yours ●

Chapter 6   SALES AND MARKETING   79
                 Introduction ● Setting the objectives ● Pricing
                 policies ● Know your consumer ● Moulding
                 your product ● Distribution ● The power of
                 promotion ● Advertising ● Packaging ● Print-
                 ing ● The value of test marketing ● Go out and
                 sell ● A sales force? ●

Chapter 7   EXPORTING   90
                 Introduction ● Market Research ● Promoting
                 your product ● Documentation ● How will
                 you get paid? ● Bridging the finance gap ●
                 Insurance ● Freeports ●

Chapter 8   PLANNING AND FINANCIAL CONTROL 100
                 Adopting a strategy ● Management accounts
                 and budgeting ● Putting costings to use ●
                 Costing capital projects ● Controlling your
                 stocks ● Stock valuations ● Research and
                 development ●

Chapter 9   OBTAINING FURTHER FINANCE   114
                 Introduction ● Mortgaging property ● Spe-
                 cialist concerns ● Government assistance ●
                 Presenting your case ● Danger signs ● Further
                 reading ●

Chapter 10   THE IMPORTANCE OF PEOPLE   123
                 Introduction ● Having the right mix ● Defin-
                 ing each job ● Setting objectives ● Looking
                 after employees ● Staff training ● Job efficien-
                 cy ●

Chapter 11   GROWING LARGER   135
                 Introduction ● Are you doing as well as you
                 could? ● Taking on a new partner ● Leasing ●
                 Factoring ● Extending or moving ● Diversify-
                 ing ● Mergers and acquisitions ● Management
                 buy-outs ● Acquiring a computer ● Going
                 public ●

USEFUL ADDRESSES   **147**

PRESENT VALUE OF £1   **153**

INDEX   **155**

To Claudette
who makes everything worthwhile

CHAPTER 1

Making a Start

You've taken the first step — to successful management of your own business. By taking advice.

You will succeed with the determination which you obviously possess, a lot of the right kind of advice and a little bit of luck, to which even Rockefeller would admit.

Perhaps you are already in business. This chapter is specifically aimed at the employed man, or woman, who has yet to make up his or her mind. To decide whether or not to take that gigantic step to going it alone.

But if you are already part of the exciting way along that road, don't skip this chapter. Use it to re-assess yourself and your changed situation. It may make your passage a smoother one.

Weighing up your present situation

Sit down and take a cold, statistical look at yourself, your job and your environment.

Break it down and take stock of all the many benefits which you currently enjoy and which, in your search for pastures new, you may be overlooking.

Your major asset will almost undoubtedly be job security although naturally this will be very dependent on your occupation. If you are unfortunate enough to be unemployed, then the security factor is irrelevant.

Do you work set hours, or, considered another way, are you fairly certain at what time your next meal will be?

This is just one of a number of 'assets' which you may have to forego if you intend to take the path of self-employment. Let us look at some of the others.

Does your job attract 'perks', such as a company car, luncheon vouchers, cheap travel or goods, or even just a subsidised canteen?

These are all worth hard cash and, if working for yourself, will have to come out of profits, your new form of income.

What about pension rights? Leaving a pensionable post is an expensive exercise if you go before the natural retiring age.

To what degree of stress are you subjected? This will without doubt increase dramatically if you work for yourself.

Perhaps you have some degree of responsibility; almost every job includes some, despite the apparent lack of it. We will assume that you want a lot more!

Your statutory rights are important and cannot be ignored in today's legislative society. Laws tend to be in the employees' favour and you will thus become subject to them instead of being protected by them if you 'change sides' and become an employer. (See Chapter 5.)

If you have a Trade Union behind you, this can prove a powerful ally in times of dispute, sickness or accident. If you become a 'boss' it may become a force with which you will have to contend.

Finally, still looking at the favourable aspects of your present job, have you ignored companionship and, possibly, congenial working conditions? Both could disappear, at least initially, if you become a 'one-man band' working in less favourable conditions.

Looking on the bright side

'If I've really got all that', you might be saying, 'Why should I risk it all to make the change?'

But then, there *are* a lot of things missing, aren't there?

Freedom of choice will be high on the list. Freedom to work in an area which appeals to you and to devote as many hours as you wish to your new business — which will be many more than you are now putting in!

To expound, and to expand upon, your own ideas becomes a refreshing incentive. To put into practice all those thoughts rushing through your head will spur you on towards your goal.

At last the decisions — and the responsibilities — will be yours. The buck will fall into your lap — and stay there.

One of the major considerations enticing people to want to work for themselves is the thought that, finally, they will be properly and more adequately rewarded for the skill and expertise they know they possess.

This is the most misleading incentive of them all.

Cash considerations should be put squarely to one side until all the remaining factors have been carefully considered and analysed. If by that stage your mind is not firmly set upon taking the plunge, don't do it.

If you allow potential financial advantages to sway you, you will almost certainly come unstuck. At some crucial point — and there will be several — your slight lack of confidence, determination or one of the other major factors will plummet you to despairing depths and set you on the road to disaster.

For this reason, money aspects are not in the main considered at this stage; they reappear at the end of this chapter.

You should now be obtaining a much clearer insight into what you really have now and what you stand to lose, or gain, by going it alone.

Write it down

The comparisons so far are naturally general and you will be more interested in your own specific case.

This is not too difficult if you have some particular line of employment in mind. This, again, can be quite wide in its scope at this point and you will soon spot 'gains' and 'losses' if you draw up a 'league table' such as the one below.

From experience I find that factory employees form a high proportion of those starting their own businesses and, quite often, their vehicle is a small store in a suburban run of shops. Let us look at these two extremes.

Factory Worker	Shopkeeper
Geographical area Mainly industrial	Perhaps of your choice?
Immediate place of work Factory	Shop
Hours worked Say 8 a.m. — 4 p.m. five days a week. Some overtime?	60/70 hours per week very likely. Certainly Saturdays and perhaps Sunday mornings. Unsocial hours.
Holidays 4 weeks annually, plus Bank holidays?	Probably none in the first few years, unless a relative stands in. Bank holidays will have to be worked in certain trades.

Factory Worker	Shopkeeper
Working atmosphere Noisy, crowded, smelly, stuffy?	Should be clean and reasonably airy. But don't forget that some of the backroom jobs may be less pleasant, e.g. cutting up bacon.
Type of work Monotonous?	Varied but certainly busy at times, boring at others.
Companionship Probably very good.	You may be on your own for a lot of the time, although customers will be there to talk to.
Responsibility/Leadership Nil or little?	Absolute!
Administration/Organisation Dependent upon responsibility	Again, very full. Book-keeping, V.A.T., P.A.Y.E., etc.
Daily Travel Car/Public Transport? Cost factor? Time 'wasted' — perhaps 30-60 minutes daily.	If you are living over the shop, no problems here.
Leisure and Lifestyle Evenings and weekends free at the present to follow social life? Enough surplus earnings to save for occasional luxuries?	Restricted, perhaps, to Sundays and half a day weekly. Remember that stock purchases have to be organised, books made up. Profits may need to be ploughed back in the early years. Some leisure pursuits will have to be abandoned.
Prospects Limited? Further qualifications needed for promotion? 'Dead men's shoes' syndrome?	Can be unlimited and subject to personal capabilities and financial resources only.

You will see that financial considerations feature only lightly in this assessment. They must be viewed more fully later and not cloud your judgement at this point.

You should now be clarifying certain criteria in your own mind and, hopefully, be approaching that vital decision whether or not to strike out on your own.

What about YOU?

It has been said that the person who works for himself is a breed apart. One who possesses certain rare qualities, many of them entirely instinctive, enabling him to survive in today's highly competitive and unfriendly, complex business world.

How are you going to know whether you are a member of that exclusive club?

We have compared above different practical facets of two occupations. Now, let's try analysing the real YOU!

No psychiatrist's couch is needed, just an unlimited degree of unadulterated honesty on your part. One person you cannot cheat in an assessment test is yourself.

Imagine you are ready to meet your maker and only perfectly honest answers to the following third-degree test are going to issue you with the passport for entry through the pearly gates, although in this case your passport — if all the stamps are in the right columns — will allow you to turn at the crossroads towards the sign reading — 'Self Employed this Way'.

Temperament

What kind of attitude do you possess? Are you easy-going, prepared to accept the status quo and somewhat annoyed when changes cloud the horizon?

Or are you eager for new challenges, ready to adapt, and accept improvements?

Leadership

Have you a preference for taking orders, or giving them? Do you find it frustrating to have to accept instructions from others when you feel that, left alone, efficiency would result if your own ideas were followed?

Do you feel competent in dealing with subordinates, or is every awkward instruction creating tension in your breast?

Could you competently deal with unsavoury decisionmaking such as the giving of notice to a colleague? Or would such thoughts be undermined by allowing your heart to overrule your head?

Willpower

If a goal has been set, is your willpower of sufficient strength to strike at achievement without wavering? To set your course and not allow minor crises to upset you?

Past personal experiences should come to mind, pinpointing your success, or otherwise, in reaching previously set goals.

'Stickability' sums up the necessary attribute here and, granting some adaptability, you should know whether you can honestly tick the 'Yes' or the 'No' column.

Confidence

This is essential. Without it, some of the other factors will lack the strength of character we seek in order to succeed.

Do you have confidence in your own ability and does this confidence come over when dealing with others, whether subordinates, peers or customers?

We all tend to sum up a newcomer in the first thirty seconds of speaking to him and it is within that vital fraction of time that you must 'sell' yourself.

Security

Are you a believer in personal and family protection, in the form of a secure salaried position, or are you ready to face insecurity in the hope that its rewards, mentally and financially, will in time be to your advantage?

This risk factor is, of course, the greatest one and for a family man or woman, there are considerations beyond one's own skin.

Health

Working for yourself produces great demands on both mental and physical resources. Can you withstand such pressures?

Stress will undoubtedly increase and there will be little time for sick leave!

Family Aspects

Husbands, wives, children all feature in the plan you have in mind; have you carefully considered each one? Schooling, holidays or a change of home may all prove upsetting and the psychological as well as the practical angle should be analysed, preferably in a 'family council'.

Expertise

Most human beings are particularly good at something and both natural as well as technical abilities should be listed.

Attributes in the manual, intellectual and organisational fields call for investigation as well as a close look at your own hobbies and interests. These can invariably provide clues as to the type of individual you are.

If you have no practical experience of the field you hope to enter, you may well be wasting your time. No amount of enthusiasm can cover up a lack of knowledge.

Have you tried working for, say, six months in a shop on a part-time basis, if you aim to enter retailing?

You will need more than technical expertise to run your own operation and several bodies today specialise in training would-be entrepreneurs in such skills as marketing, planning, personnel and finance.

The Business Education Council runs a series of courses for people interested in being in charge of their own concern, whether it be a restaurant, a manufacturing outfit, or, indeed, any commerical enterprise.

In the case of would-be shopkeepers, you would be taught the principles of buying, display, book-keeping and so on.

Three different courses cater for those with less than four 'O' levels or C.S.E.'s, those with four or more, and for students with one or more 'A' level.

Alternatively, some forward-looking universities (Durham is one) are setting up internal business schools in collaboration with the Training Services Agency. Eighteen-week courses are available for managers who wish to set up their own business. The Open University also runs a 'Start Up Your Own Business' course based upon work books, audio cassettes and video tapes, and covers marketing, financial and production techniques. Students will be allocated to an adviser for up to nine months and will have to make a presentation, at the end, of their business plan.

Catering for all tastes are the Manpower Services Commission's New Enterprise Programme, its Small Business Course and its Self-Employment Courses.

The first of these is especially designed for people who are determined to set up a new business which will quickly grow into a sizeable venture. A comprehensive grounding in business strategy is provided by each of the Glasgow, Durham, Manchester, Warwick and London University Business Schools. Each programme runs for about 4 months and the principal elements covered include:

How to present your business idea.
The need for a business plan.
Researching the market.
Costing, pricing and selling.
Forecasts, budgets and cashflows.
Raising funds.

The Small Business Courses are shorter (6-10 weeks) and are run for the M.S.C. by universities, polytechnics, colleges, regional management centres and private consultants. All costs are met by the Commission which also pays a weekly allowance to participants.

Self-Employment Courses are aimed at men and women who want to earn their own living rather than setting up business ventures; i.e. 'one-man bands'.

All three types of course are available only if you are 19 or over, unemployed or willing to give up your job and have not been in full-time education for at least two years. Disabled people may be able to avoid some of these conditions.

Application can also be made to the M.S.C. to benefit from its Management Extension Programme, which provides a small business owner with a seconded, experienced manager to help with the development and implementation of a project likely to lead to the firm's growth or an improvement in its fortunes.

A very successful innovation has been the Government's Enterprise Allowance Scheme whereby a weekly grant of £40 for a year is paid to unemployed people who set up their own business. Applicants must have been out of a job for at least 13 weeks and receiving unemployment or supplementary benefit. They must also be in a position to raise £1,000 themselves, if necessary by borrowing it.

Whatever type of business you have in mind, make a determined attempt to gain grass-roots experience of its basic principles before you commit yourself. This could be the best move you ever make.

Summing Yourself Up

You should now have a much clearer picture of the real YOU. Having stripped the social varnish from the somewhat different exterior that we all tend to exhibit in today's rat-race climate, you should be left with your genuine qualities and abilities.

Whilst there is probably no such entity as the ideal entrepreneur, you are certainly going to need generous helpings of the following ingredients:

Determination

Crises there will be in abundance. Only strength of character will pull you through. Goals must be set and nearly all else thrown to the winds in the determination to achieve them.

Self-employment is not for the faint-hearted, nor for the easy influenced where a safer path becomes available.

Grit and a certain degree of dogmatism must be your cornerstones; never let them crumble.

Practicability

This you will almost certainly already possess. Now prepare yourself for an abundance of planning, setting down, achieving and then more planning.

Everything you do must have an air of confidence about it. Be practical in every decision, however small, for it is in the sum of dozens of minor decisions that success will come about.

One of Henry Ford's early decisions was at what price level he would aim to sell — and look what he achieved.

Judgement

Linked with the practical nature of your approach will be your own evaluation of things. How you arrive at your decision will be partly inbred but more importantly influenced by your own experiences.

For that reason don't expect to make correct decisions every time. But do make a decision; self-employment is not for the 'fence-sitter'.

If it proves erroneous, but salvageable, your business may suffer a little but your experience will have widened. Next time your judgement will be that much more precise.

Enthusiasm

Sackfuls of this will help you through but the other assets you will need are not enough alone without a mixture of zeal.

Everything must be done with a song in your heart, even when you feel down. There is no time for the 'blues'.

Enthusiasm tends to be contagious and if you are building a team around you your energy will rub off as a bonus to the united effort.

Hard work there will be aplenty, but an enthusiastic frame of mind will ease it along.

Flexibility

Although a determined path must be followed, an adaptable approach is vital in the light of changing events.

The market may swing in a different direction, a new product could arrive or government interference may affect your attitudes. Be ready for — and don't be afraid of — change.

Diversification normally involves a major upheaval but there will be, along the line, opportune moments for re-analysing your methods.

If outside factors indicate the advantage of a swing of emphasis, make your move boldly. Don't wait for your competitors; by then it may be too late.

Integrity

Most businesses grow from within, i.e. satisfied customers come back for more, and, in time, recommend your product or service to their friends.

Such continuity demands an absolute faith on their part in your integrity.

Faulty goods will have been instantly, and unquestionably, exchanged. Mediocre service will have been investigated and corrected. Only by these methods will your clientele grow. We all know what happens to a business that gets itself a bad name. Your insistence on placing your customers on a pedestal must filter through to the rest of your organisation, however rapidly it grows. An insolent telephonist or an uncaring receptionist could be the first death-knell of what you thought was an efficient organisation.

Humanity

People's feelings have to be considered and this includes staff as well as customers. Treat staff like the human beings they are and they will react in similar vein towards the signatories of the cheques, those people providing the monthly lifeblood of your business.

Deal with them shabbily and inevitably their own feelings of frustration will filter through to your customers to the detriment of the business.

These are seven vital elements in your own make-up which will help you to succeed. Pin a list of them on the desk before you, and remind yourself, from time to time, of their importance. When problems arise, use them to help you analyse the reasons, and you will surprise yourself how often a crack in one of them will turn out to be the real culprit.

Taking Advice

Research, research, research. Let that be your motto, and one of the best ways of adding to your increasing store of knowledge is to talk over your ideas with other people.

Two heads are without any doubt better than one and the more heads you take advantage of the better.

Speak to friends, relatives, and neighbours. Bounce ideas off them. You will be surprised how rewarding this exercise can be.

Ask people to be absolutely frank, even brutal. If the same criticism of one of your suggestions keeps recurring, it will need a re-think. Value the fact that you are probably talking to potential customers.

Your Bank Manager

He is the ideal springboard where your bouncing can begin. He will normally be quite prepared to chat in general terms, at an early stage, prior to your putting a specific proposition to him as outlined in Chapter 3.

His advice will not be restricted to finance and you will quickly discover he will have local knowledge of many industries and services. His opinions should therefore be valued.

If you do feel you are not getting your money's worth from this source (although remember the advice is free!), then shop around the clearing banks until you feel you have struck up the right relationship.

People in the Trade

You will no doubt have a general idea of the line you intend to follow and some specialised advice can be sought.

Speak to people in the trade or profession of your choice and test their reactions. You need not tell them all your ideas and of course you will need to balance their advice against the fact that they may prove to be direct competitors.

If you have retailing in mind write to the National Union of Small Shopkeepers of Great Britain and Northern Ireland. They have 10,500 members and will provide helpful advice.

Similarly, most occupations liaise through a trade body and proper enquiries should soon reveal the source you require.

Some areas have special advice centres for people about to embark on a business. In Islington, for instance, there is the Action Resource Centre (staffed by, among others, Marks & Spencer executives), whilst Enterprise North is operated on Tyneside by Durham University.

Small Firms Information Service

This is a Government sponsored organisation set up to advise both new and established businesses through various offices in England, Scotland and Wales.

A series of first-class leaflets ranging in titles from *Starting a Business* through *Obtaining a Franchise* to *Starting a Manufacturing Business* are obtainable free of charge from the centres.

Use Your Library

Most large libraries have ideal reference sections staffed by competent and helpful librarians who will willingly point you in the right direction for further advice.

A general browse through a good reference library will reveal all sorts of useful ideas and information. Specialised additional facts can then be ascertained with the librarian's assistance.

Chambers of Trade and Commerce

These tend to deal with already established businesses but sometimes staff will help, providing you aim specific rather than general questions at them.

Professional Advice

This may be too early to appoint a legal adviser or even an accountant, although if you are in the fortunate position of knowing such experts, make use of their advice.

Chapter 5 deals more fully with your choice of such advisers.

Weighing it all up

You should now have a portfolio of ideas, suggestions and information and very soon that magical decision of throwing up your present job will have to be made — or abandoned.

The cash considerations we have left until the end. If you are still unsure at this stage, stick with what you have got. Don't let the financial implications swing your decision one way or the other.

If you have made up your mind to go it alone, allow the money side merely to consolidate your decision. Things will be financially tight in any case, but providing your determination and careful research have convinced you of your potential, you will survive those hard-up patches.

Whilst you may have read or heard many times that Britain does not do enough to encourage the self-made businessman, the opposite view is taken by some notable — and highly successful — entrepreneurs.

The managing director of a firm making medical laboratory products, set up only eight years ago and now thriving, has gone on record as saying that this country is a Utopia for the man (or woman) determined to go it alone.

The Money Angles

Bear in mind your current *true* income. Add back the 'perks', if any, be they luncheon vouchers, company car, or a non-contributory pension fund.

Certain deductions can be made, such as the cost of travelling to work daily if this is to be eliminated. Meals out may no longer be an expense if accessibility to home cooking is part of your plan.

Compare the adjusted figure with your potential self-employed income. This is not easy to calculate but however you measure it, take a severely pessimistic view.

A recently introduced inducement for the newly self-employed may help. Providing you are not forming a limited company (see Chapter 5), any losses in the first four years (which are not unusual) may be set off against your last three year's tax paid as an employee.

Paying your wife a salary for assistance rendered will bring the tax bill down but remember that anything you do pay her still has to come out of profits!

So far we have considered income, but your capital will also be put at risk.

Any savings will undoubtedly be needed to finance the initial step. Are you prepared to lose them?

A small mortgage may give way to a larger one, a more modest house may have to suffice and even the family car may become a van, all in the plan to achieve your dream of self-employment.

Your mind is made up. Now let us take your particular choice of occupation and learn in much greater depth how to investigate your intended market.

CHAPTER 2

Investigating the Market

Introduction

Before you jump off into unknown worlds, discover as much as you possibly can about *your* particular product or service.

It is impossible at this stage to find out *too* much. The greater your store of knowledge, the easier your gradient to success will become.

In this chapter we look at the ways and means of researching your subject to enable you to see how *your* enterprise will fit into the current economic scene. We are going to study the *environment*.

How wide an appeal will your idea have? Is it something — such as Blackpool rock — that will have a limited geographical market, or is the potential on a national, or even international, scale?

What is the current consumption? Is it, like bread, widely bought or, like silver presentation tankards, a now-and-again item?

Is it cheap or expensive? If the latter, then its appeal is going to be limited to the better-off. Thus you may be unwise to set up your stall in an area of heavy unemployment.

How specialised are you aiming to be? Bicycle clips are sold, although the buying fraternity is a dwindling one.

Is design an important factor? Or packaging? Many manufacturers, aided and abetted by modern department store techniques, have learned how vital it is to catch the public's eye. 'That looks nice' aimed at a packaged cake is merely a compliment to the artist, but it sells the cake.

A dull package has few chances of selling and this applies as much to a retailed item as to a poorly finished or badly boxed engineering part.

Is your product a bulky one and thus restricted to the able-bodied, or is it conveniently carried and readily grasped by today's instant shopper?

Some parts of the country, like Manchester where it is known as the Group 20 Foundation, have special bodies to seek out products suitable for manufacture by small firms.

Take a close look at your intended consumer. Might this person, who is going to pay your wages, be of either sex — or is yours a strictly male or female line? If it is either of these, you have immediately cut out about half of the population as potential customers.

Are you looking to a particualar age range or even social group? The more narrow your limits, the smaller your market share prospects become.

How long will your product last? If it is guaranteed for 10 years, don't expect many repeat sales.

Does it have a second-hand market? Whilst this can promote further new sales, it again restricts your potential since many people will prefer, or only be able to afford, the cheaper, once-used article.

Convenience is a consumer by-word today and a complex tool is likely to do as badly as a cafe on top of a hill with no road!

Ignore the economists and make your own predictions about future prosperity — or the lack of it. A medium-term (1–3 years) view is all that may at first be needed and this should provide you with another clue as to your own prospects for growth. Your viewpoint is as good as anybody else's in what is now only a guessing-game. A local as well as a national outlook is needed if you anticipate serving the needs of the community around you.

Finally, look closely at any technological advances in your intended field, as well as the rapidity of these. Progress may quickly overtake you!

This is a general insight into the environment surrounding your future life; a more detailed survey should be taken along the lines of the statistical section appearing later in this chapter.

Don't forget the Competition

This is one aspect where your research will already have overlapped.

In looking sweepingly over the market as a whole, future competitors will have become quickly obvious. Don't be put off; let your emergence give *them* some sleepless nights.

Are you entering a highly competitive field, or working on a fresh idea? Either course will bring its problems. Competitors are no gentlemen and will sacrifice some of their profit margin if they feel you should be eased out of the firing line. Equally, few ideas can be entirely copyrighted and a successful one will be chased by abundant imitators.

Competition cuts prices and whilst the companies concerned may grumble, legislation normally ensures that the consumer wins.

Measure local as well as national competition and don't overlook the market share which mail-order, through catalogues and the Press, now takes.

Would you be competing like with like or with the 'big boys' of the trade? They will have established their business the hard way and over a period where their experience cannot be matched, however enthusiastic you may be. Do not imagine that you are going to put them out of business!

If your idea is an entirely new one — although remember the old adage that there is nothing new under the sun — have you checked to ensure that someone else is not also working along the same lines and may beat you to the starting post?

This is not an easy task of course. Trade periodicals can assist and, studied over a period, may provide clues as to new designs and new thinking.

Medicinal breakthroughs, in particular, have a habit of coinciding, often in widely diverging parts of the world. Technology invariably advances side by side in similar conditions, despite differences in innovators or location.

Lastly ask yourself the question — 'Why should I do any better?' There may be a hundred and one apparently valid answers, but analyse each closely and be as certain as you can that *your* product or service will be a step ahead of the field.

Cost Considerations

The consumer still gets what he pays for and there will always be those willing to pay that little extra for something better. Hence with most goods and services a wide range of prices is available.

Whilst one man is unprepared to pay more than say £10 for a pair of shoes, another will find five times this sum for a better product.

Although income has a bearing on such variations in choice, personal priority plays almost as important a part.

The man with the £10 shoes may think nothing of spending £3 or £4 several evenings a week in a social club; his £50 footwear neighbour may consider this an extravagance.

For the suppliers, these varying priorities provide a wide range of markets. Do not be over-concerned, therefore, if your particular commodity is going to cost more than the competition, providing you are confident there are consumers willing to part with extra monies for a quality item.

Attempt a reasonably detailed breakdown of similar goods already on offer. You will no doubt have some idea of their material cost, the labour element where this is appropriate and you can hazard a guess as to the necessary administrative overheads.

How large is the factory or shop concerned? What might the rent be? The number of employees times the average wage in the industry will provide the labour bill, and so on. Do not overlook capital costs, nor depreciation of fixed assets.

Such an exercise will not prove easy and may not always be appropriate but, where it can be calculated, the results should be useful to you.

Look at the entire price range and try to locate at what level your idea will appear. Imports may look a lot cheaper but measure the quality. The consumer will, in due course, be measuring them against yours.

Labour intensive articles will invariably be more expensive than those where material costs are more in evidence, although automation is helping to balance these out. Stronger union representation will demand a greater proportion of turnover. Intricate items may involve heavy design costs and these may recur in a market influenced by fashion. Research and development costs can also prove to be a hidden, non-productive element.

Seasonal businesses must have a built-in subsidy factor to make up for a lower out-of-season turnover.

If you intend to grow, cost your product on eventual overheads rather than early, less expensive ones. Larger premises, increased administrative costs and perhaps wider advertising may swamp your present profits, forcing you to push up selling prices to the level of your competitors. At that stage your initial flush of success will have died a premature death.

Before deciding on a growth path, don't overlook your limitations. A man can labour for only so many hours a day and if you intend to set up as a window-cleaner, this will limit the number of windows you can clean!

Similarly, aim only at a practicable share of the total market; monopolies are still outlawed. One man who moved into ball bearing manufacture based his first year's output on a figure which turned out to be 80% of the total U.K. consumption!

Something called elasticity of demand will affect your product or service, according to whether it is a luxury or a necessity. It is said that bread sales would not fall dramatically if the price were doubled overnight; a much greater proportional fall in output would certainly result in a similar price increase in such luxuries as whisky or foreign holidays. Bear this in mind when considering price increases.

Seasonal influences

Brief reference has already been made to the 'subsidy' factor but there are other important points to consider where you are not going to be fully operable throughout the year.

Staffing can prove difficult and although seasonal work is accepted as normal in holiday areas, it may not always be easy to supplement your labour force during busy periods elsewhere.

There is often an abundance of part-timers available in a heavy unemployment period, although these may not necessarily be of the quality you require. The work may be skilled and such capable people normally expect full-time employment.

'Seasonal' can apply as much to time of day as time of year and here again staff problems are not unknown. Where unsocial hours need to be worked, a premium may be demanded not allowed for in your otherwise careful costings.

Weather remains uncontrollable and do not bank, therefore, on sales of summer goods merely because it is July or August! You may wish you had stocked up with galoshes instead of sun hats!

Timing is vital in a new seasonal occupation and it would hardly be businesslike to set yourself up as a seaside hotelier in October. Similarly, do not leave production of Christmas gifts, if that is your line, until November, by which time orders will have been placed.

Cash flow becomes somewhat more chaotic in seasonal production and forward planning is essential. The inevitable off-season troughs must be covered.

Your personal life will not remain unaffected where a seasonal occupation exists. Blackpool landladies, for instance, get quite used to the idea of holidaying in November,. and if you are offering an emergency drain cleaning service, don't expect to be joining the Bank Holiday crowds on the way to the sea!

One advantage of seasonal work is the opportunity for diversification. Deck-chair operators offer winter chimney-cleaning services, whilst one businessman sells boats in the summer and domestic organs in the winter, the power sources for both being manufactured by the same Japanese company!

The Uncontrollables

However carefully you lay your plans, external factors may upset them. Although outside your control, nevertheless you should be aware of these influences.

Legislation can be the most damning, and overnight your opportunism may become illegal. Government controls can be introduced in any sector considered necessary by Parliament and your scheme can be thwarted.

Local legislation, delegated by Ministers through, for instance, bye-laws, cannot be overlooked and can often by quite frustrating to your potential business.

Planning permission can, of course, be checked in advance but changes in attitude by local councils cannot be forecast. Ventures such as swimming clubs in home pools have been legislated against in their prime.

Remember that licensing is normally in the hands of local officials and this extends to such activities as bus services and the transportation of heavy goods by road.

Be alive to local and national feelings towards your particular type of business and ignore only at your peril potential antagonism or illwill by those in authority. Sudden legal intervention, such as has occurred on the gambling scene, can chop the profit potential almost overnight.

Governments can also change their minds, as the giant North Sea Oil combines have found to their cost in being obliged to pay higher rates of taxation.

Import subsidy changes have less effect in today's international trade but cannot be forgotten and a wary eye should be kept on Press reports.

Trade journals provide the latest recorded information and, as already stressed, those affecting your venture should be continually and thoroughly analysed.

New roads, motorways or airports can all alter trade situations in the areas affected and even early rumours of these should be investigated. Your local planning office is the base to start your enquiries.

Self-employment must, by its very nature, contain a high risk element and whilst such uncontrollable factors cannot all be catered for, their possible intervention must remain uppermost in your mind. Any which seem appropriate and potentially damaging (or advantageous) must be given priority in your research.

(See also Chapter 6.)

After the Sale

To make a sale — of a commodity or a service — to a customer is only the first link in a new relationship. It must not end there.

You will, of course, be satisfied. But will the customer?

Is the article going to be satisfactory, and ideal for his purpose? Will he consider it a 'reasonable buy' or a 'best buy'?

You must be satisfied at achieving nothing less than the latter. Not only do you want that client to call again; you want him to recommend you to his neighbours, his friends, his relatives.

To retain his goodwill, you must be ready to deal with any complaints, spontaneously and efficiently. Not only ready, but able.

This is where many new businesses flounder, particularly in 'middle-men' firms, i.e. those dealing in already manufactured goods.

The law of averages indicates that some percentage of those goods will not be to the customer's satisfaction.

When this happens, your ability — your willingness is assumed — to put the matter right promptly will determine whether that customer will call again, or shop elsewhere.

Do you maintain enough stock to provide an instant replacement? Or is the poor customer kept waiting, for days or weeks, whilst you obtain another?

In a line of articles requiring eventual repair, your capability either to undertake such repair or point the customer in the right direction will again influence his choice of supplier when a replacement is needed. Make certain he comes back to you.

Never attempt to ease your way out of guarantee terms; unless completely inappropriate, accept full responsibility and put the matter right. Although legislative moves continue to favour the consumer, making direct and indirect suppliers of unsuitable or faulty goods liable, taking on the moral responsibility will maintain the goodwill of your customer.

Any legal protection you do feel it necessary to draw up should never be done without speaking to your solicitor first.

Communication difficulties can become pronounced where follow-up service is required. To have to retrieve one or two damaged items out of a delivery of several hundred to a customer, many miles distant, will present its own special problem. You must be prepared to handle such difficulties. Bus tour operators faced with a coach breakdown will know the feeling!

After-sales service will naturally depend on the product or service offered and may vary from negligible (selling tins of beans or manufacturing spoons) to complex (selling motor cycles or making watches).

But its importance must never be overlooked and, if necessary, some contribution towards its cost must be built into the original price.

Finding Out More

The amount of information you will require before embarking any further will be related to what you intend doing.

If your eye is on a local corner shop only parochial issues need be investigated, although the degree of thoroughness should be no less than if you are setting up a manufacturing concern in a highly competitive field and aim to cover the entire country.

In this case, however, statistical information is available and a careful study of this will help you to assess future planning. What are the major sources of such information?

Trade Associations, if applicable, are your first port of call, whether it be the Booksellers Association, the National Union of Small Shopkeepers, the Society of Beauticians, the Caterers' Association, or whatever. The National Allied Societies will put you in touch with the appropriate body if you are unsure. Chapter 5 lists umbrella organisations.

Some, such as the Hotel & Catering Industry Training Board, offer a Small Business Service especially aimed at people like you.

The Small Firms Service operated by the Department of Trade & Industry is designed to improve the availability of information and advice to small firms. In-depth advice is available from the Service's business counsellors (themselves mainly experienced businessmen) who can provide sound, practical, impartial and confidential guidance on any kind of business enquiry whether it relates to developing a going concern or starting from scratch.

The Service can assist in drawing up a plan, raising the necessary funds, choosing the right premises, marketing, and so on.

You are entitled to three free advisory sessions after which a £30 fee is charged for each subsequent session. There are over 80 counselling offices around the country. Call 'Freefone Enterprise'.

A Technical Enquiry service is also available to help with minor problems relating to manufacturing techniques and organisation. Questions such as 'What is the best material to use for this job?' and 'How can I improve production methods?' can be answered on a confidential basis.

Where an extremely thorough survey of the current market seems appropriate, the Market Research Society will recommend member firms able to undertake this task. Extensive reports are available but naturally these can be expensive although the £1000 or so could prove very well spent. Technological entrepreneurs would be well advised to consider this service. The British Institute of Management also offers a Consulting Services Information Bureau, which publishes *Guidelines for the Small Business*. Some first-class local organisations exist to help with market research such as 'Local Eyes'.

The specialised Press should be studied and this can be done at no cost whatsoever at major libraries. The *Writers and Artists Year Book* and *Willing's Press Guide* list the more widely read publications.

The library can also be utilised to research *Which*, the Consumers Association magazine, regularly reporting on many products and services.

'Business Monitors' is a service of the Department of Industry, publishing monthly, quarterly and annual reports based on information collected regularly by the Business Statistics Office. Over 30,000 concerns, in the manufacturing and mining section alone, report back, thus providing very wide coverage.

These monitors follow business trends, the progress of individual products and seasonal factors, and enable businessmen to assess their own performance against the norm.

Everything from bedding to electrical engineering and jewellery to valve manufacture are in the ranges covered, and data include types and numbers of businesses operating, personnel engaged, turnover, purchases, floor space, stocks, credit sales and capital expenditure. The reports are not expensive and can be ordered from H.M. Stationery Offices.

The Government Statistical Service, the overlord in these matters, also produces a great number of books available to the general public, again through H.M.S.O.

A list is published and titles vary from *Summary of Figures for Caterers* to *Family Expenditure Survey,* mostly reasonably priced.

The G.S.S. brochure also contains an invaluable summary of 'contact points' within many Government departments and lists telephone numbers, with extensions where appropriate.

Numerous directories exist for those wishing to find out more about companies already in existence. Some of the key directories are:

(a) *Directory of Directors* (all directors of the principal public and private companies in the U.K.)
(b) *Jordan Dataquest Ltd.* (financial information on 40,000 companies in the fields of electronics, office equipment, data processing and chemicals)
(c) *Guide to Key British Enterprises* (alphabetical listing of 20,000 prominent companies, along with their 'vital statistics')
(d) *Major Companies of Europe* (Vol. 1 EEC, Vol. 2 Non-EEC; 6000 of the largest companies)
(e) *Kelly's Directories* (various classifications)
(f) *Stock Exchange Official Year Book* (all quoted companies are detailed)
(g) *Who Owns Whom* (U.K. Edition) (a directory of parent, associate and subsidiary companies)
(h) *Kompass U.K.* (a registry of British industry and commerce)

Several company information services are also available, including the following:

McCarthy's Company Information Service
Moodies British Companies Service
Extel British Company Card Service

Annual reports of public companies can be obtained from the appropriate registrar or from the Companies Registration Office in

Cardiff, where private company accounts also have to be filed.

Credit-rating agencies will supply confidential status reports, as will the banks. The latter also issue useful statistical information through such brochures as, for instance, Lloyds Bank's *Economic Profile of Britain*, updated annually.

Subscribe to *Small Business,* obtainable monthly from W.H. Smith's, and published by the Small Business Bureau. Also of interest may be *Venture Capital Report,* a monthly journal about entrepreneurs which provides a method for reaching many potential investors quickly. A number of other publications now exist to serve the small business community, such as:

Your Business	(Centaur Publications)
Venture U.K.	(Redwood Publishing)
First Voice	(Nat. Fedn. of Self-Employed & Small Businesses)
In Business Now	(Dept. of Trade & Industry)

although you may find others have taken their place, for such magazines tend often to live fairly short lives.

There are also available such means of advice as the *Business Opportunities Digest* and business starter publications specialising in one particular field. Business Publications Ltd., for example, offer no less than 20 'Start a Business' books, from *Newsagents* to *Dating and Marriage Bureaux.*

More enlightened areas have founded their own Business Clubs where regular meetings are attended by those wishing to make a start as well as by successful entrepreneurs. Meetings are usually structured to provide members with an open forum to thrash out business pitfalls, to promote their own products and services and to gain first-hand experience from fellow members.

Providing invaluable assistance throughout the country are the many Enterprise Agencies, now under the one umbrella of Business in the Community (B.I.C.). It has ambitious plans for growth which incorporate promoting its agencies and beefing up some 27 community action programmes fostered by the C.B.I.'s Special Programmes Unit.

B.I.C. is supported by some 100 companies as well as by government departments and local authorities.

There are over 200 Enterprise Agencies and almost certainly one near you. All sorts of enquiries are dealt with by experts, who often include seconded bank managers. The accountants, Deloitte, Haskins & Sells, have an excellent free booklet on these Agencies.

By now you should be well armed with a wealth of information relating specifically to your choice of business. These facts and figures at your fingertips should help to guide you along the rocky path, and ensure that mistakes are few.

The deskwork, however, is over. The practical work is about to begin. Let us now get down to the real task of setting you up in a business of your own.

CHAPTER 3

Finding Start-Up Money
and
Using it Effectively

Introduction

At the end of the day, the provision of the finance necessary to get your idea off the ground will prove to be the most vital consideration.

If adequate capital is forthcoming, it will enable you to concentrate your mind on other matters connected with starting your business. If you cannot raise the necessary finance, I am afraid you will have to continue being nice to your present boss!

But these are two extremes. There can be nearly as much danger in raising too much cash as too little. The former may encourage you to be too ambitious whilst the latter, although giving you the impetus to start, may stop you in your tracks at just the wrong moment.

Before you go any further, therefore, it is imperative that you cost your project as accurately as possible.

How to Cost Your Project

Initially, there will be two major considerations. The first will involve the acquisition of — and payment for — certain capital items.

Merely having a base may mean the purchase of a building, be it factory, warehouse, shop or office. It has to be fitted out and perhaps renovated, or at least decorated.

'Fixtures and fittings' is the loose term used by accountants to incorporate all such 'additions' to buildings and includes shelving, display material and items of furniture.

Larger acquisitions and generally ones which are expected to show a return on their use, will come under the heading 'Plant and

Machinery'. This includes all types of industrial machinery and, for instance, usually larger refrigerators and freezers which tend to retain some inherent value. Fixtures and fittings, on the other hand, unless rather special, are normally written down to nominal values in Balance Sheets since, invariably in a bankruptcy or liquidation, they fetch next to nothing.

Vehicles will be a further important capital necessity for most businesses, although these will vary from a small, second-hand van to a larger lorry.

Also demanding some of your finance will be the running costs of your business, known as 'working capital'.

This is the term for the sum needed to generate enough steam to run your project until that magic day arrives when your customers start sending you cheques — although a working capital need will still continue.

Labour will have to be paid (even *you* cannot live on fresh air for very long), materials or stock bought and other 'running' overheads met.

Important considerations at this period of calculating your total financial need will be the periods of credit taken from your suppliers and given to your customers.

Imagine, for instance, that in the line of business you are undertaking it is normal for suppliers to give you one month's credit although you may be unlikely to receive payment for goods or services supplied for double this period.

Within this two months, obviously certain payments will have to be met although, fortunately, most services, such as telephones, electricity and gas, will not have to be paid for until a full quarter has elapsed. Rates demands may not drop on your mat for perhaps six or even twelve months.

You can see from the example below that wages — be they your own and/or your employees' — will constitute the major outgoing during that vital first two months.

Example

Going into business manufacturing small machined parts and employing two machinists might produce a full costing as follows:

	£
Premises (rented, 3 months rent in advance)	500
Installation of electricity, phone, etc.	200
Machinery (deposit only; remainder on hire pchse.)	500
Tools (provided by customers)	–
Material (1 month's supply; 1 month on credit)	200
Sundry workshop/office equipment, stationery, insurance, etc.	200
Vehicle (second-hand)	1000
Vehicle running expenses	200
Your own living expenses	800
Employees' wages	1800
Hire purchase payments	200
Total	5600

To this must be added something for unknown costs and emergencies; the delivery van may break down on its second day. Certainly in this example you should be looking at a total cost of at least £6,000.

Your own Stake

How much of this total are you going to have to find yourself and how much can be financed from other sources?

If you can meet the total requirement from personal savings, all very well, although remember that you are still borrowing for the machinery through the hire purchase company.

Friends or relatives may assist with capital although this can present problems at a later date if, for instance, repayment is requested for some reason unforeseen at the outset. Such folk may also expect some say in running the business, which may be unacceptable to yourself.

We discuss the best way to approach a clearing bank later in this chapter but if this is going to prove necessary the bank will normally be expecting you to put in an acceptable stake. So in this example you should certainly need to lay your hands on, say, £2,000.

Preferably this stake of yours should not be borrowed or you may find financing the repayments on so many sources of funds too heavy a commitment on your new business, strangling it before it gets very far.

You may have held a life policy for several years which can be surrendered for cash, but this should be a last resort and certainly linked with replacement cover for any dependants. Security is dealt with later.

Anticipated profits should allow for all forms of borrowing to be repaid in the shorter term, say within three years. Longer-term finance at this early stage should not be contemplated unless the business demands heavy capital commitments and, in this case, profit margins will need to be above average to balance the additional risk factor.

How to Raise Finance

There are only a limited number of institutions in the U.K. which look kindly on the businessman-to-be.

Clearing Banks: Primarily the major clearing banks (Barclays, Lloyds, Midland and National Westminster) provide the majority of these funds, catering for both asset acquisitions and working capital needs.

Borrowing may be arranged on an overdraft or loan basis although it will be the bank manager who will decide. Overdrafts are usually a little less expensive and you are charged interest only on the amount borrowed from day to day. Charges will vary between, say, 2½% and 4% over the bank's Base Rate which can fluctuate and is linked to interest rates generally.

Whilst overdrafts are usually agreed for one year, with a review to follow, loans may be granted for longer periods, possibly up to five years although more generally for two or three years for new businesses. For both overdrafts and loans the actual interest element will normally be charged to the account quarterly or half-yearly.

Hire Purchase: Hire purchase or finance companies provide many new businesses with the assets they need although borrowing by this method is more expensive than a bank facility.

Interest is added at the outset at a 'flat' rate, the true cost being nearer double the quoted figure. The reason for this is that a 10% flat rate on a one-year loan for £100 will cost £10 in interest charges, but since the £100 is not being borrowed for a full year but is being repaid, probably on a monthly basis, the real rate being charged on the actual amount borrowed is nearer 19% p.a. This is referred to as the 'annual percentage rate' or A.P.R.

Hire purchase is suitable for a wide range of goods including vehicles, machinery and equipment, providing the item is an identifiable one, has a life expectancy in excess of the loan agreement and commands a good second-hand market.

Any such asset so hired is treated as owned by the hirer for tax purposes and full capital allowances given (where appropriate) in addition to the interest payable being allowed against profits.

All the major clearing banks have hire purchase subsidiaries and your bank manager can put you in touch if he feels unable to assist through his normal channels.

Leasing: Leasing is gaining popularity, particularly for business vehicles, although any identifiable asset may be leased.

The asset remains the property of the leasing company, qualifying it for capital allowances which can be reflected in lower rentals. The concern leasing the article, however, can charge these rentals to pre-tax profits. The rental period is usually anything from 3 to 5 years, although with the gradual phasing out of capital allowances, this form of finance may become less attractive.

Although almost any item, from typewriters to aircraft, can be leased, this method of finance is in the main reserved for growing, established concerns and for this reason is expanded upon in Chapter 11.

Other Sources of Finance:

Insurance Companies: Industrial or commercial properties can sometimes be purchased over, say, 10 to 15 years with monies provided by one of the major insurance companies but they will only consider 75% or so of a forced-sale valuation of the property involved.

Investors in Industry (Known as 3is): This Government encouraged company, run by the major clearing banks and the Bank of England, assists smaller and medium sized companies through its subsidiaries, Industrial and Commercial Finance Corporation (I.C.F.C.) and its Ventures Division.

I.C.F.C. will consider smaller applications although its average loan is nearer £100,000. Ventures starts at £200,000. Ventures concentrates on innovative ideas and welcomes an opportunity to review technical developments in any sphere. It also involves itself on occasions in the management of companies in which it invests.

I.C.F.C. is currently advancing some £500m to nearly 4,000 companies. Your bank will be able to put you in touch if the manager considers you have a case.

Merchant Banks: These are not normally a source of finance for other than established businesses, and are merely mentioned here to prevent entrepreneurs from being otherwise disappointed if an approach had been considered. See, however, Chapter 9.

Agricultural and Rural Sources: Farmers are a special case and comparatively well looked after financially by the Agricultural Mortgage Corporation and the many feed and fertilizer merchants eager to forge links with potential customers.

The Council for Small Industries in Rurual Areas (CoSIRA) provides advisory, consultancy, training and credit services for small firms in England (employing usually less than 20 people) in the £250 to £75,000 range, and will also grant building and equipment loans.

In Scotland there is the Small Industries Council for Rural Areas in Scotland and the far north is served by the Highlands and Islands Development Board. The latter offers similar services to the other bodies but will consider grants and loans up to £400,000.

Development Bodies: Scotland and Wales have their own Development Agencies which look favourably at new businesses and will assist with as little as £2,000. Northern Ireland is served by its own Agency, and loans are also available there from the Local Enterprise Development Unit.

In Ireland the Industrial Development Authority operates to attract manufacturing concerns and is able to boast that its rate of corporation tax will not exceed 10% for the remainder of this century. The Irish also promise that free repatriation of profits and dividends will continue. A 100% depreciation allowance is granted on all plant, equipment and buildings.

The English, Scottish and Welsh Tourist Boards make grants towards capital costs and sometimes, exceptionally, will help with loans. All types of tourism projects, including improvements to hotels, leisure amenities, self-catering projects and tourist support facilities may be eligible but they must:

> involve capital expenditure and provide a tangible asset; grants are not given towards running costs or replacements; be open to the general public without discrimination; be substantially for the benefit of tourists, as opposed to the local people; have at least outline planning permission; and *not* have started before the Tourist Board has made a formal offer of a grant.

Assistance will be the minimum necessary for the project to proceed. Most grants are in the 20% to 30% range and the total assistance for a single project from public-sector funds (including, for instance, the Countryside Commission or any other Government body) will not normally exceed 50%.

The three Tourist Boards and the British Tourist authority provide a wide range of promotional and development services and they may make contributions to the cost of domestic marketing initiatives and studies.

Petrol Companies: Potential garage owners will find that petrol companies offer attractive financial packages, often for up to ten year periods and without any interest charges. Breweries offer similar schemes.

Government Grants: These are not always as easy to lay your hands on as the Government agencies would have you believe. Having said this, however, it would be sensible to pursue this avenue just in case your

If they can do it, so can you.

FLAVERCO LIMITED: "It had to be Central Lancashire because nobody could equal the cost advantages they offered."   MR. S. GRIMSHAW.

L. C. AUTOMATION: "Our company is rapidly expanding. Central Lancs. give us the flexibility to do it easily."   MR. J. HUTCHINSON.

You've got a good idea and you're bursting with enthusiasm. But going from an idea to a viable business is a big step to take. One that's too big to take on your own.

So before you do anything, get in touch with us, the Central Lancashire Development Corporation.

Because, like the successful businessmen above, you'll find we can give you far more than just floor space.

We can also offer the right unit in the right location, and scope for expansion as business grows.

But more importantly for the new businessman, we can offer attractive lease terms which will ease the pressure of starting up a new business.

So if you're looking to get your idea off the ground, contact Bill McNab, Commercial Director, at the address below.

Central Lancashire
A BETTER PLACE TO BE

CENTRAL LANCASHIRE DEVELOPMENT
CORPORATION, CUERDEN HALL, BAMBER BRIDGE,
PRESTON PR5 6AX. TELEPHONE: PRESTON (0772) 38211.

particular idea qualifies and for this reason grants are expanded upon in Chapter 9.

From time to time the Government makes some very worthwhile offers but they invariably operate on a 'first come; first served' basis, and you have to be quick to spot them. Engineering firms with less than 200 employees, for instance, can occasionally qualify for non-repayable, one-third grants towards the cost of high technology machinery.

The *Investors Chronicle* regularly publishes a detailed source list of available finance, and you would be well advised to obtain the latest issue which contained this information.

The publishers of this book also produce annually the *Sunday Telegraph Business Finance Directory*, now recognized as the prime guide to sources of corporate finance in Britain. The guide contains numerous entries, fully cross-indexed as well as a number of helpful articles to get you under way.

Other sources include Irex, a computer-based exchange via which people with ideas can contact people with capital.

The Prince of Wales is encouraging promising new products or processes and has lent his name to an award worth £10,000 to the winner. There are few restrictions on entry and the Engineering Council will provide details.

Government Guaranteed Loan Scheme

Introduced on a trial basis in 1981, this scheme has proved exceptionally popular although remains under Government review.

Lending is in the hands of the many banks and financial institutions operating the scheme, but the Government underwrites 70% (formerly 80%) of any losses. Borrowing is rather more expensive than through traditional means and the current premium is 5%.

The maximum which may be borrowed is £75,000 and repayment can be arranged over between 2 and 7 years. Sole traders, partnerships, co-operatives and limited companies are all eligible although some activities are excluded, principally agriculture and horticulture, finance services, estate and travel agents, tied public houses, bars and night clubs. Business assets must normally be pledged.

Over 14,000 businesses (both established and start-ups) have been assisted to the tune of over £450m in total.

The failure rate, not surprisingly, has been high — perhaps one in three, of participating firms. Against this, however, can be measured many success stories and, although minimal, a number of new jobs have been created up and down the country.

Ask your bank manager for details.

Business Expansion Scheme

This scheme was introduced in 1983 to encourage individual outside investors in providing risk monies for unquoted trading companies. Tax relief at the individual's highest rate (i.e. normally 60%) is available providing the investment remains undisturbed for five years.

So if you can find a rich uncle (but not father, mother, son, daughter or spouse!) to inject up to £40,000 (each year if available) into your business, you can both possibly benefit. There are some restrictions and your accountant's advice should first be sought. Tax leaflet IR 51 is also helpful.

A large number of professionally-managed B.E.S. funds now operate and several million pounds have been collected from individuals and injected into companies in this way. Both start-ups and established businesses can qualify.

Agriculture and property development are excluded.

Approaching Your Bank Manager

This should be a pleasurable rather than a nail-biting time for, hopefully, you will receive free advice, encouragement and possibly an offer of financial assistance.

Much will depend on your line of approach. Wander in without an appointment with scrappy pieces of paper littered with figures and you are just as likely to receive a flea in your ear. Your bank manager is a busy man but will, nevertheless, welcome you providing you have the courtesy to let him know beforehand when you will be calling and you arrive at his desk properly armed — in the financial sense! However, it is not only finance that he will want to discuss with you.

He will want to be assured that you have the appropriate experience or, if this is new ground you are covering, that your research has been thorough and your idea appears a viable one.

If you are considering the purchase of a newsagency and had not considered what time in the morning your feet would have to touch the ground, this will not inspire much confidence.

Be completely open and honest, for you will certainly be found out if you don't tell the whole story — warts and all.

Let us assume that you have a good tale to tell and you appear to be convincing him. What else will he require?

Certainly a cash projection is the finest tool at this stage that you can have in your workbox; this is discussed later.

You will already have produced your costing of the venture and perhaps a glint of approval is now appearing out of the bank manager's eye. If you can produce enough of the right kind of collateral — he will call it 'security' — the money may be yours.

Don't necessarily expect an instant decision. You have probably spent weeks on research, give your bank manager a few days to do his homework. See also Chapter 9.

Types of Security

Naturally if the purchase of buildings is in your plan, then you will have some ready-made security. Don't think, however, that if a factory is to cost you £25,000 the Bank will lend this sum against the deposit of the deeds.

Banks have what they call 'lending values', these being their assessment of the amount of cash they will lend against such security. A table giving guidelines, which remain flexible and can vary with a firm's credit-worthiness, follows this section.

Plant and machinery are not looked upon too kindly as collateral and neither are vehicles. Fixtures and fittings quite definitely are out.

Limited companies can secure their borrowing in the form of a debenture, a particular variety of mortgage. The debenture can 'pick up' fixed assets such as land, property and debtors (monies owing to the company) as well as floating assets like stocks, work in progress and cash.

Directors of a limited company may be asked to give personal guarantees, certainly in the early stages of borrowing. The bank may feel that if it is asked to have faith in the company, i.e. a separate legal entity from the directors, then the latter in turn should back the bank's faith.

Sole traders and partners may offer as security mortgages or second mortgages over their own homes, life policies, stocks and shares if held, or building society funds.

Some third party, whose financial standing can be verified by your bank, may offer his guarantee and this invariably provides adequate security in smaller figures for newly formed businesses.

Lending Values

This table must be treated with great caution and it must not be forgotten that, as well as varying according to customer, different banks adopt differing percentages.

Commercial and Industrial buildings 50% – 60%	less prior
Private residences 66% – 75%	mortgages
Stocks and shares 50% – 60%	('Gilts' even more)
Debtors 50% – 70%	less preferential creditors
Stock 10% – 25% normally	
Life Policies	full cash surrender value

Keep Your Bank Manager in Touch

Don't skip away elated at obtaining your overdraft or loan, never to visit the Bank again. Make your bank manager your constant adviser and confidante.

Maintain a close eye on your cash projections and, after amendments, send — or better still, take — a revised copy to your bank. Explain the reasons behind discrepancies and your optimism — or pessimism — for the future.

Always be one stride ahead of your bank manager. Never make him telephone you — beat him to the call. If you know that your account is going to be a little more stretched than envisaged, tell him why.

Your banker is an avid writer. Every conversation you have with him will be faithfully recorded.

How much better for your file note to read 'Mr. X telephoned to warn of a cheque he had drawn which might take him £100 over the agreed limit. I told him that this would be in order', than 'I had to telephone Mr. X as his account was £100 over his limit; I warned him that I might not pay his cheque next time.'

Make a habit of keeping in touch — at least every 3 or 4 months, and more frequently if your busines is going through a sticky patch.

Cash Projections

Simply, these reveal the flow of cash coming into and going out of a business and for this reason are often referred to as 'Cash Flows'.

They should be distinguished from Profit and Loss Accounts and Balance Sheets for they are concerned solely with cash and no other item. Remember that cheques are cash!

Projections are tabled chronologically, normally month by month. Heading the table will be cash received from sales and any other sources and from this sub-total will be deducted all cash payments due.

At the foot of each monthly table will be the cash balance forward and, month by month, the running — or aggregate — situation at the bank, either credit or debit.

Projections must be regularly scrutinised, reconciled with the true situation as shown on bank statements and amended as anticipated payments and receipts become actual. The position may improve or worsen but either change must be analysed to discover the reasons.

When compiling your flow chart, remember that goods invoiced out to customers on, say, 31st January and not normally paid for until two months have elapsed should show as cash receipts for April, for this is the month in which the money will probably reach you. Always attempt to show the worst situation.

A typical Cash Projection will look like this:

Scrambled Eggs Limited

Receipts	Jan	Feb	Mch	Apl	May	June
Cash sales	100	100	100	100	100	100
Cash from debtors	800	600	800	800	800	800
Rent received	20	20	20	20	20	20
Building Society Interest	100					
TOTAL:	1020	720	920	920	920	920

Payments	Jan	Feb	Mch	Apl	May	June
Cash purchases	60	60	60	60	60	60
Creditors	400	300	400	400	400	400
Wages/Sals. inc P.A.Y.E./N.I.	160	160	160	200	160	160
Rent/rates			50			
Telephone		30			30	
Elecy/Oil			30	60		
Vehicle running expenses	20	20	20	20	20	20
Repairs/renewals		60				
Bank/H.P. charges	20	20	20	20	20	60
Policy premiums	10	10	40	10	10	10
Taxation						40
V.A.T.			180			180
Accountancy charges		60				
Sundries, postage	10	10	10	10	10	10
TOTAL:	680	730	970	780	710	940
Net debit		10	50			20
Net credit	340			140	210	
Bank balance (800 debit (overdraft) b/fwd)	460	470	520	380	170	190

The opening overdraft of £800, although after the initial fall appearing to show a worsening situation, in fact improves to show borrowing of only £190 at the end of the period.

If the forecast had not been planned, some undue worry might have crept in during March.

Six months is a reasonable period for such a chart to cover; any longer only means more guesswork. Remember to make allowance for five-week months if wages are paid weekly.

Note that a cash projection differs in several important respects from a Profit and Loss Account and does NOT, in fact, reveal a profit forecast. Depreciation of assets, for instance, is ignored, as are any adjustments to stock values. Remember, also, that the figures are shown as at the end of each month and further fluctuations can occur from day to day.

I.C.F.C. produces a useful booklet entitled *Profit and Cash Flow Forecasting*; free from their London office.

Costing

This topic more than any other seems to frighten off the small businessman. He is more interested in the production of his article than the correct costing of it and whilst many successful entrepreneurs rely on their 'noses' to arrive at a selling price, today's fierce competition underlines the necessity to ensure that each item is properly costed to provide a *guide to pricing*.

Inflation, also, decrees constant costing reviews and the bankruptcy lists are full of firms that relied on outdated overheads. Today's product must be costed allowing for today's expenses.

Some basic knowledge of costing is therefore essential and it is only the underlying principles that we shall look at here. In Chapter 8 we shall see to what uses your costings can be put.

First segregate your fixed and variable costs to give yourself an indication of the additional expense incurred in producing one more item; this is known as marginal costing.

Example
To manufacture 1,000 widgets a company has to meet the following expenditure:

Fixed Costs	£
Rent, rates, heat, light, phone	
Administration	550
Machinery — finance costs	
Depreciation	
Variable Costs	
Labour	
Materials	450
TOTAL	1000

Whilst each widget costs exactly £1 to make, to turn out one more might cost only 45p since the fixed costs may not vary and have already been catered for in the manufacture of the 1,000 items. This argument cannot, of course, be extended *ad infinitum* since a stage will be reached when the fixed costs will have to rise to cater for the increased production.

There are thus two major bases for costing your product; either 'total cost' or 'marginal cost'. With the first, all known costs are allowed, whilst with the latter only the variables are assessed.

One method does not give you more profit than the other and only by comparing the two will you discover which is the more practical for your type of business.

It is also important to distinguish between direct costs (which can be identified with a particular product and which may be fixed or variable) and indirect costs (normally fixed overheads which, in a multi-product concern, would not be easy to allocate to each product on a fair basis).

Having arrived at a standard cost for any particular unit, whichever method you adopt, you will then be able to compare this with actual costs once your 'production line' is running. Costing, of course, is just as important in a service industry as in a manufacturing one.

Any differences revealed between standard and actual costs are known as variances and, from detailed analyses as to whether, for example, these are material, labour or overhead variances, you will know where adjustments in expenditure or prices may have to be made.

Material costs are usually the easiest to calculate (remembering to allow for wastage, etc.) but labour and overheads present more problems.

Example
If you pay a production employee £2.50 an hour, much more than this will have to be charged out to your customers as this table shows:

		Hours p.a.
1 man × 40 hours per week (exc. lunch)		2,080
Holidays (3 weeks)	120	
Bank Holidays (10 days)	80	
Sickness, say 6 days p.a.	48	
Unavailable hours		248
		1,832
Allow, say 10%* inefficiency		183
		1,649

$$\text{Real cost per hour} = \text{Rate} \times \frac{2,080}{1,649} = \text{£3.15 an hour}$$

* In practice this may be much higher.

Example

	£
Total annual overheads, say	10,000
Add depreciation	500
Total costs to be recovered	10,500

Total productive hours (as before) 1,649
Overhead recovery rate = $\frac{£10,500}{1,649}$ =   £6.37 an hour
(2 men will halve this and so on)

Note. Neither of these examples allows for a profit margin which will again have to be built in to the rates charged. So the total charge of a job lasting, say, 4 hours will look like this:

	£
Material cost, say	20.00
Labour: 4 hours × £3.15	12.60
Overheads: 4 hours × £6.37	25.48
	58.08
Profit margin (before tax), say 15%	8.71*
	66.79

If your profit calculation is made this way, don't overlook the fact that it represents a lower percentage of the selling price, in this case 13%.

Keeping Records

It is, of course, essential to maintain proper records of a business and invariably one of the faults behind an ailing concern is a lack of proper regard for books of account.

Your accountant will advise you what records need to be maintained and these should present no great problem. The major ones will be:

Cash Book: To record all cash entries, including cheques and postal orders, both in and out. A typical page would appear thus:

Receipts		Ref.	£	Payments		Ref.	£
2 June	Sales	4	120	14 June	Stock	5	80
30 June	Rent received	6	20	30 June	Wages	10	200
2 July	Sales	4	100	2 July	Creditors	3	140
4 July	Sales	4	800	14 July	Electricity	12	26

The reference numbers are cross-referenced to the appropriate ledger so that, for example, all stock purchases are recorded in more detail (including the name of the supplier and probably his reference number) in Ledger Number 5.

The Cash Book should be balanced either weekly or monthly, and reconciled with the bank statement, making adjustments, for instance, as follows:

				£
31 August	Cash Book balance forward		Credit	920
September	Receipts	1,200		
	Payments	800		
				400
				1,320
Add cheques not yet presented at bank				150
				1,470
Deduct credits not yet received by bank				200
Bank Balance			Credit	1,270

Sales and Purchases Ledgers: These may be contained in two separate account books or by sets of cards, one for each customer and supplier. Dates, details and amounts should be recorded as soon as they are received or paid out.

Asset Records: The cost, and current valuation, of all assets should be recorded for Balance Sheet purposes. This, of course, includes stock. An appreciating asset, such as property, will be revalued only from time to time, perhaps every 5 or 10 years.

Sundry Records: V.A.T., and P.A.Y.E. and National Insurance payments should be maintained and recorded, as well as Petty Cash items.

You will save yourself money with well-kept records for, apart from their obvious use to yourself, your accountant's charges will be that much lower if your books are easily understood.

Credit Control

Taken in its widest sense, this term embraces control of all your customers' dealings with your business and it begins before you accept their order.

New businessmen are often tempted into taking orders from whatever source and this should be avoided. Remember that you will be parting with your own goods to possibly a stranger and allowing him, 1, 2 or even 3 months before you know whether or not you will receive any money. Think of it as an unsecured loan. Very few concerns do not have some bad debts.

Intending customers seeking credit should offer trade and bank references and these should always be followed through. Enquiries can also be made of trade protection societies and do not be put off from taking some precautions, even with 'big' names. Remember Rolls Royce! Set credit limits where appropriate; these can remain flexible, but they do provide a useful discipline.

Bank replies are invariably vague but your manager will probably give you a clearer definition of what they really mean.

Your firm's literature must be clear as to terms of payment and this should also be shown on invoices, e.g. 'Cash in 60 days'.

If two months is normal in your particular trade, after that period draw up a list of debtors still outstanding with name, amount and date of invoice. This should then be closely monitored, at least weekly, and followed up with statements, reminder letters, telephone and possibly personal calls according to how desperate the situation appears. There is no golden rule except to keep chasing your money. (The publisher of this book publishes *Credit Control Letters in 15 Languages* containing examples of the necessary letters.)

Consider insuring your debtor's monies with a major firm like Trade Indemnity Credit Insurance, who specialise in this sort of thing.

If legal action seems necessary, weigh up the cost involved as, of course, there is still no certainty that you will be paid. Small claims may be pursued through the County Court but solicitors' costs may prove too onerous in other cases. The use of a reputable debt collecting agency should be considered, although ensure you know the full charges before you instruct them.

Finally, if you feel that giving discounts will mean more rapid turnover, calculate the real cost (especially if you have an overdraft at the bank) and bear in mind that many large companies will still deduct your offered discount even when paying *after* the discount period has elapsed!

A useful guide to credit control is published by the British Institute of Management, free to members.

Budgets

Every business should work to a plan. How else will you know whether progress is being made — or even a profit?

Since budgets are estimates, some assumptions have to be made. You may allow, for instance, a 15% increase in sales, a 10% increase in the wages bill, a rise in overheads of 8% and a material cost uplift of 5%. All these projections will be built into your budget to give estimated results.

A budget does *not* show the cash situation; this has been dealt with earlier in this chapter. It should, however, allow for inflation.

It should run for, say, six or twelve months (no longer) and be updated regularly. Monthly tabulations are sufficient for most businesses and these should be kept as simple as possible. Combine sundry expenses and do not show such individual items as postage or electricity unless these take a relatively large proportion of your income.

Example

Welsh Rarebit Limited

	1985								1986			
	May	Jun	July	Aug	Sep	Oct	Nov	Dec	Jan	Feb	Mch	Apl
1 Sales	1000	1000	1100	1200	1200	1200	1000	800	600	800	1100	1200
Materials	200	200	220	240	240	240	200	160	120	160	220	240
Labour	200	200	220	240	240	240	200	160	120	160	220	240
Direct costs	100	100	110	120	120	120	100	80	60	80	110	120
2 Cost of Goods	500	500	550	600	600	600	500	400	300	400	550	600
3 Gross profit	500	500	550	600	600	600	500	400	300	400	550	600
(1 less 2)												
Admin. exp.	100	100	100	100	100	100	100	50	50	100	100	100
Selling, dis.	100	100	100	100	100	100	100	50	50	100	100	100
Other o/hs	50	50	50	50	50	50	50	30	30	50	50	50
4 Total o/hs	250	250	250	250	250	250	250	130	130	250	250	250
NET PROFIT	250	250	300	350	350	350	250	270	170	150	300	350
(3 less 4)												

Note: Profit is, of course, shown before tax. More detailed use of Budgets is expanded upon in Chapter 8.

Break-Even Charts

A Break-Even chart is another useful tool to combine with your Budget. It will show you at what sales volume you will begin to make a pre-tax profit. See example on next page, along with an explanation.

Example Break-Even Chart

Firstly, break your expenditure into fixed and variable costs.

Fixed costs:	Rent, rates, heat, light, ect.	£1,000
	Administration costs	400
	Selling expenses	340
		£1,740

Selling price per unit, say,	7
Variable cost per unit (material, labour)	4
Contribution towards fixed costs	3

To meet the fixed costs, therefore, you will need to raise £1,740 divided by £3 = 580 units. At this point the business will just break even, showing neither a loss nor a profit. This can be shown on a chart and, extended, will reveal the potential profit or loss at any given volume of units (see top of opposite page).

Note that total costs are made up as follows:

Fixed costs	£1,740
Variable costs (580 × £4)	£2,320
	£4,060

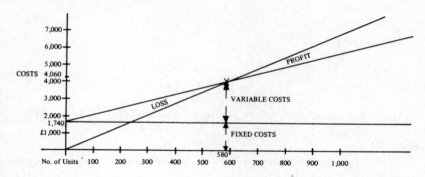

Useful Ratios

Some yardsticks should be adopted to gauge the progress of your business. It doesn't really matter whether the basis you use for these is strictly in accordance with text book standards as long as you use the same formula each time. This will then provide you with a useful trend which can be plotted to show a continuing situation. Peaks and troughs will soon reveal themselves.

Dozens of such ratios exist but at this early stage a handful will suffice. They are split below between performance, i.e. how well the business is doing, and liquidity, a measure of cash or 'near-cash' assets.

Performance Ratios

(1) $\dfrac{\text{Profit}}{\text{Capital employed (or net assets)}}$ e.g. $\dfrac{£1,000}{£12,000} = 8.3\%$

This is known as the Return on Capital and is used for all sizes of business. Profit should be calculated before taxation and any interest payments on long-term funds. The capital employed figure, you will find, is the difference between the assets and liabilities of your business, i.e. net assets.

The resultant percentage will naturally vary from one type of concern to another and in a business which needs a lot of capital assets will be smaller than one which operates on few assets. One figure you may compare with your Return on Capital is the before-tax interest you could earn on your money if it weren't invested in your business.

(2a) $\dfrac{\text{Gross Profit}}{\text{Sales}}$ e.g. $\dfrac{£800 \times 100}{£4,000} =$ 20%

(2b) $\dfrac{\text{Net Profit}}{\text{Sales}}$ e.g. $\dfrac{£200 \times 100}{£4,000} =$ 5%

(2c) $\dfrac{\text{Overheads}}{\text{Sales}}$ e.g. $\dfrac{£600 \times 100}{£4,000} =$ 15%

These figures will tell you how efficiently you control your costs and prices. You will see from the examples above that if overheads rise to 18%, this will leave a net profit of only 2%

(3) $\dfrac{\text{Annual Sales}}{\text{Stock}}$ e.g. $\dfrac{£4,000}{£300}$ = 13 times p.a.

The more often you can turn over your stock, the more profit potential rises. A drop in stock turnover may indicate slower selling lines for reasons of obsolescence or non-competitive pricing.

Liquidity Ratios

(4a) $\dfrac{\text{Current Assets}}{\text{Current Liabilities}}$ e.g. $\dfrac{£3,000}{£2,000} = 1.5$ or $1\frac{1}{2}$ to 1

This ratio should normally be better than 1 to 1 (in manufacturing it may need to be nearer 1.5 to 1) and a lower balance calls for investigation before cash flow problems emerge.

(4b) $\dfrac{\text{Current Assets less Stocks and Work in Progress}}{\text{Current Liabilities}}$

e.g. $\dfrac{£1,800}{£2,000}$ = 0.9

This is known by accountants as the 'acid test' since it excludes assets that are not reasonably quickly convertible into cash. Since some current liabilities (e.g. taxation) may, on the other hand, not be immediately called for, the resultant ratio should ideally be about 1 to 1.

(5a) $\dfrac{\text{Debtors}}{\text{Sales (Annual)}}$ e.g. $\dfrac{£600 \times 365}{£4,000} = 55$ days

(5b) $\dfrac{\text{Trade Creditors}}{\text{Purchases (Annual)}}$ e.g. $\dfrac{£700 \times 365}{£3,000} = 85$ days

These are measures of credit given and taken respectively and will naturally vary from trade to trade. Again, trends are more important than solitary figures and an upward swing in the period taken by your customers should warn you to chase debtors more actively.

Note that only *trade* creditors are included in (5b) and that the cost of purchases, rather than the sales figure, is used.

Taxation

Although this is something which may not concern you immediately, the subject cannot be avoided for too long!

If your business has been set up as a sole proprietorship or a partnership, you will be subject to income tax on the profits made in the same way as an ordinary employee would be on his income. Note that it is on the profits and not your own drawings that the tax is levied since, if a proportion of the profits is to be left in the business, this can have an adverse effect on cash flow.

Special rules exist to determine the basis of taxation during the first three tax years of a business and thereafter tax becomes due on the profits of the preceding year. Any early losses can be carried forward to offset future profits prior to calculating the tax due. Ask at your tax office for 'Starting in Business' (IR. 28), a very useful guide.

Limited Companies pay Corporation Tax, currently 30% p.a. on profits earned of under £100,000. See also Chapter 5.

Your accountant will tell you what can and cannot be deducted from turnover before reaching a taxable figure but in the main, apart from obvious costs such as materials and labour, these are as follows:

Deductible:
Advertising costs
Bad and some doubtful debts
Rent and interest payable and other running costs
Business insurances
Legal expenditure (including costs of raising finance)
Redundancy payments (up to statutory maximum)
Repairs to premises

Not deductible:
Expenses not wholly and exclusively incurred in running the business
Abortive capital projects
Domestic and private expenditure
Taxation of any kind
Improvement to property
Travel to and from business
Entertaining, unless the visitors are from overseas

Following the major overhaul of company taxation in the 1984 Budget, reliefs and allowances are, in the main, gradually being phased out. Rates of corporation tax, on the other hand, are being correspondingly reduced with an aim to boosting profitability in all sectors. Writing down allowances, as explained below, will remain.

The current position is as follows:

Plant & Machinery: A proportion of the total cost may be deducted from profits in the year the asset is acquired on the following basis:

Expenditure incurred on or after 1 April 1985: 50%
Expenditure incurred on or after 1 April 1986: Nil

There are very few exceptions to this new rule and your accountant should be consulted *before* you commit yourself to any major purchases.

Having taken advantage of any first year allowance, the residue may be written down by 25% p.a. until it disappears. Plant or machinery sold or scrapped within about 5 years of acquisition (providing this is after 31 March 1986) may be 'depooled' and written off over the shorter period.

Vehicles: Business vehicles, such as vans and lorries, fall into the 'Plant & Machinery' category above. For cars there is no first-year allowance, but they may be written down at 25% p.a. on the reducing balance, up to a maximum of £2,000 for any one car. Where a vehicle is used for both private and business purposes, the allowance is accordingly reduced on a pro-rata basis.

Industrial Buildings: As with Plant & Machinery, although the rates are somewhat different:

Expenditure incurred on or after 1 April 1985: 25%
Expenditure incurred on or after 1 April 1986: Nil

There is also a writing down allowance but in this case, it is at 4% p.a. of the original cost of the building. These allowances do not apply to shops and offices.

Enterprise Zones (see Chapter 4) remain exempt, and you will thus still be able to claim 100% tax relief on all new buildings in these areas.

Initial allowances on agricultural buildings and hotels are to be withdrawn but the writing down allowance of 4% p.a. will apply.

Patent rights and 'know-how': These can be written down at 25% p.a. of the reducing balance.

Stock and Work-in-Progress: Whilst in the past several ingenious (and complex) schemes have been in operation to provide methods of relief, these have now been swept aside.

P.A.Y.E. and National Insurance

If you operate as a sole trader or partnership and you have no employees, you can ignore P.A.Y.E. If, however, you operate as a limited company then, as a director, you will be subject to P.A.Y.E. and N.I. contributions on any money you draw from the business unless it is repayment of a loan or a dividend.

Where a new employee is taken on, form P.46 must be completed unless a P.45 from any earlier employment is produced.

Certain thresholds determine rates of National Insurance payable and, at a very early stage of employing others, you should seek advice of your local office.

V.A.T.

Replacing purchase tax, V.A.T. was introduced to bring the United Kingdom into line with the Common Market and applies to both goods and services, with some major exemptions.

During each three-month period, V.A.T. charged to the business (input tax) should be compared with V.A.T. charged to customers (output tax) and the difference either paid over to or reclaimed from Customs and Excise.

Providing you anticipate an annual turnover of over £19,500 you must register for V.A.T. purposes and, additionally, if your turnover is less than this figure and you expect to be charged input tax, you will have to register to obtain repayment.

V.A.T. is currently chargeable at the following rates:

Zero (or nil): There is no V.A.T. on the majority of food items (unless served), books, newspapers, fuel, houses, young children's clothing, certain medicinal items and exports.
15%: This is the rate charged on all other items.

Customs and Excise officers will visit your business from time to time to ensure that correct recording procedures are in use. You will normally find them most helpful and their knowledge can assist you in maintaining the records required by law.

Annual Accounts

As soon as is practicable following your first full year in business, the appropriate accounts should be drawn up with the assistance of your auditor. In practice he will do most of the work although you will save him time — and yourself money — if your records are well maintained.

The annual accounts will comprise a Balance Sheet and a Profit and Loss Statement. The former is a list of the assets and liabilities of the business on a certain date, i.e. a kind of photographic record. Because it relates to one day only and is produced probably a few months later, it is of historic interest only, although once a few years' Balance Sheets are available a trend can be deduced.

The Profit and Loss Account will cover a whole year and, hopefully, record a profit made during that period.

Items relating to that year will be included whether or not payment has been received or made. Work completed and sold, but not yet paid for, will therefore be shown as 'debtors', whilst work completed, but unsold, will be included in the 'stock' figure.

Similarly, if rent, rates or similar expenditure has not been made, but nevertheless has accrued at the year-end, then these items will be reflected in the figure for 'creditors'.

There is thus a vital difference between the Profit and Loss figures and the cash situation of a business.

A typical Balance Sheet is shown below.

Example Balance Sheet

Mashed Potatoes Limited
as at 31.12.84

Fixed Assets	£		£
Land & Buildings: freehold	15,000	Capital	2,000
leasehold	3,000	Reserves	2,000
Plant & Machinery	4,000	Profit & Loss A/C	22,400
Fixtures and Fittings	500		
Motor Vehicles	5,000		
Investments	1,000		
Goodwill	1,000		
Current Assets		**Current Liabilities**	
Cash	—	Bank overdraft	2,000
Debtors	5,000	Creditors	4,000
Stock	2,000	Hire purchase	1,000
Work in progress	400	Current taxation	1,000
		Dividend	500
		Directors' loans	2,000
	36,900		36,900

Note: This is a simplified version; the law requires certain other points to be shown.

The Profit and Loss Account for the same company for the year ended 31st December, 1984 might appear thus:

	£	£	£
Turnover (sales)			60,000
Salaries, wages	20,000		
Materials	25,000		
			45,000
Gross profit			15,000
Rates		2,000	
Electricity		1,300	
Telephone		400	
Insurances		200	
Hire Purchase		200	
Car expenses		200	
Advertising		300	
Bad debt		200	
Bank and audit charges		400	
Depreciation		2,000	
			7,200
Net profit			7,800
Taxation			1,500
			6,300

This is obviously an established company which has retained its profits to build up a useful Profit and Loss balance.

Note that taxation is well under 30% and this would be due to writing-down allowances on assets; quite often the profit which a Company shows differs from its taxable profit due to such adjustments.

Some of the ratios discussed earlier are looked at below in relation to the above figures:

Return on Capital = $\frac{£7,800}{£28,400} \times 100 = 27\%$

Note that Capital incorporates *all* funds that the Company is utilising and includes here its Reserves, aggregate Profit and Loss Account and directors' loans.

Stock turnover = $\frac{£60,000}{£2,000} = 30$ times per annum

Working Capital = $\dfrac{£7,400}{£8,500}$ = 0.9

Note that directors' loans are excluded since the directors are unlikely to treat these as current liabilities.

Credit given = $\dfrac{£5,000}{£60,000}$ ×365 = 30 days

Credit taken = $\dfrac{£4,000}{£25,000}$ × 365 = 58 days

Note that the full creditors figure is used here as Balance Sheets rarely differentiate between trade and others; in practice the directors would know the figure to use. The *actual* Purchases figure should also be ideally used here rather than the cost of materials for the year.

Sources and Uses of Funds

Some accountants incorporate a Sources and Uses of Funds statement in the annual accounts and this again can prove useful for forward planning. Such a table shows where cash has originated during the period under review and the uses to which it has been put. (See below.)

Example Sources and Uses of Funds Statement

Sardine Sandwiches Limited
Sources and Uses of Funds
Year to 31.12.84

Sources of Funds	£	£
Net profit before tax	3,000	
plus depreciation	1,400	
Increase in creditors	3,300	
Sale of fixed asset	1,000	
Increased hire purchase	1,800	
TOTAL		10,500

Uses of Funds

Increased debtors and stocks	6,000	
Fixed asset purchased	2,500	
Repayment of Loan	1,000	
Tax paid	1,500	
TOTAL	11,000	
Shortfall borrowed from Bank		500

This reveals that the profit, to which has been added back depreciation since it is a non-cash debt, was boosted by £1,000 from the sale of a fixed asset and £1,800 was borrowed on hire purchase. An additional £3,300 was owed to creditors.

This total was used to pay tax, repay a loan and acquire further fixed assets. But after financing extra stocks and debtors, there was a £500 shorftall which had to be borrowed from the Bank.

CHAPTER 4

Getting the Business Going

Finding Premises

A base is something you must have, whether it be a study at home or a new factory.

Working from home is, of course, cheap, but check your lease or local bye-laws to see if permission is required. Many authorities ban home-based businesses, even if you are not annoying the neighbours.

Mary Quant started in a bedsitter, although obviously many businesses demand more appropriate surroundings.

If you have a choice of area, consider the Government's 'Areas for Expansion' scheme. Providing you are able to set up almost anywhere, but decide to plump for one of these sites, cash and other assistance might come your way.

The country is divided into Development and Intermediate Areas.

If you are a manufacturer the Government will give you grants towards the cost of new buildings, plant and equipment purchased for use in Development areas. Developments or projects anywhere in the assisted areas can also attract Selective Financial Assistance. Although public houses and shops are not eligible, such assistance is available both to manufacturers and certain service trades.

More comprehensive details are provided in Chapter 9.

The 1980 Budget introduced Enterprise Zones in areas of urban decay and the concept has since grown whereby over two dozen such Zones now exist. The benefits of setting up business in these restricted areas are enormous and include:

No rates are payable for 10 years
Exemption from Development Land Tax
100% allowances on capital spending on industrial and commercial buildings, although this relief can be clawed back if you sell within 25 years.
Exemption from Industrial Training Levies
Simplified planning

PC10	PC25	NP122

NP155	NP270

NP271	NP402	NP500

Canon suggest some useful numbers to try when looking for a good copier.

If you're looking for a copier, one of the numbers above is guaranteed to put you in touch with exactly what your business needs.

Canon's range of plain paper copiers not only offer you all the up to date developments, but also our established reputation for simplicity, efficiency and reliability.

Though each copier has its own impressive list of features, several important ones come as standard. Like the ability all our machines have to copy on plain paper or overhead projector film.

Other features you'll find on most of our copiers are enlargement and reduction, automatic exposure and the facility to copy in up to three colours.

So find out which of our copiers matches the little number you have in mind for your business, Dial 100 and ask for Freefone Canon to arrange a demonstration.

Canon
We'll help you look good on paper.

MANUFACTURERS OF CAMERAS, CALCULATORS, COPIERS, COMPUTERS, ELECTRONIC TYPEWRITERS, FACSIMILE AND MICROFILM

No Industrial Development Certificate is needed
Speedier administration
Less Government forms to fill in.

Currently there are Enterprise Zones in the following areas:

Arbroath (Tayside)	Milford Haven
Belfast	North East Lancashire
Clydebank	North West Kent
Corby	Rotherham
Delyn, Clwyd	Salford
Dudley	Scunthorpe
Dundee	Speke
Flixborough (Glanford)	Swansea
Gateshead	Telford
Hartlepool	Trafford Park
Invergordon	Tyneside
Isle of Dogs	Wakefield
Londonderry	Wellingborough
Middlesbrough	Workington

The state-owned English Industrial Estates Corporation provides a number of garage-sized units in the Assisted Areas, whilst several local authority bodies offer rent-free factories for two years, cheap European loans and free advice.

Gaining impetus in the U.K. is the American concept of Science Parks as a means of helping the growth of high technology companies. Normally based on a University, small concerns can benefit from such on-site facilities as bio-engineering, computer sciences, micro-engineering and robotics. The Department of Industry will tell you if there is such a Park in your area.

All local authorities have been asked to cut planning delays and speed up permissions for small firms. You no longer need permission to change from light industrial to warehouse use, or vice versa, for premises of under 235 sq. metres. Planning applications need not be submitted for industrial extensions of up to 20% of the original size of your buildings, subject to a maximum increase in floor area of 750 sq. metres.

Industrial Expanison Teams offer a free, confidential advisory service to help you decide where you can find the most favourable conditions. They will arrange site inspections and tell you about labour supply, transport, power, etc.

Those activities which can benefit include manufacturing and construction, as well as offices, research and development units and all service industry undertakings. The latter includes transport and communications, the distributive trades, insurance, finance, professional and scientific services.

All but manufacturing and construction, however, must provide at least 25 new jobs in the area to qualify. Projects serving primarily local needs, e.g. retailing, do not come under the scheme. Grants may be given for buildings, as well as for plant and machinery and for moving staff. Firms operating in the Areas for Expansion are given preference when tendering for Government contracts.

New London businesses are looked after by the London Enterprise Agency, backed by two of the Clearing banks and Marks and Spencers, amongst others. A former television factory in Lambeth is being converted for use by up to 50 companies, and marketing and accountancy skills will be provided as well as help towards running costs. Small businessmen seeking premises in the West Midlands are especially catered for by the County Council who are developing workshops from as little as 600 sq. ft. upwards.

Members of the National Federation of Self-Employed and Small Businesses are entitled to consideration of a mortgage scheme operated by City of Westminster Assurance for individual advances of £10,000 to £25,000 over 20 years. In any case, always approach your local authority, for many are sympathetic towards new businesses that are likely to create job opportunities in their area. Mortgages are often provided in this way.

A useful free service is run by the Location of Offices Bureau for firms considering setting up offices anywhere in the country. Availability of space, staff and housing is recorded as well as details of grants where appropriate.

If you are going to manufacture, enquire whether an application for an Industrial Development Certificate is needed, basically for buildings over 50,000 sq. ft. in non-assisted areas and 15,000 sq. ft. elsewhere where there is I.D.C. control. Even if you do not require one initially, bear their existence in mind. Your initial choice of location could hamper later expansion plans.

The Government is also providing 1,000 new Nursery Units for industrial expansion in conjunction with private industry in the Assisted Areas.

You must decide between renting or building and a correct decision here is vital. There are factors other than cost to consider, such as ensuring that the building is ideally suited, and sited, for your needs.

Cost will vary according to region, location, the condition of the building and access. Renting, as opposed to buying or building, will have a completely different effect on initial outlay as well as on cash flow. Rents vary enormously and in London for instance can be double those of Wales or the North-West.

Your own building may normally be modified later but, against renting, a large proportion of your capital will have been permanently tied up.

The correct type of building is important and a professional survey is always recommended. Ensure that the basic structure is sound, and look at maintenance and repair possibilities.

Are the facilities to your liking? Will the staff be happy? They certainly won't be if two rickety flights of stairs have to be negotiated before they can 'spend a penny'!

Is the wiring adequate? Your electricity board will gladly check this for you. Look at all the mains services and consider heating, ventilation, air conditioning if necessary, and also telephone and telex availability.

The Department of Energy will pay £75 towards a survey (almost all the cost) to establish where wastage may be taking place under an Energy Survey Scheme for small and medium-sized firms.

British Gas, through its Technical Consultancy Services, will advise on installations and suitable training courses on fuel management. Solid fuel users can look to the National Coal Board for similar help.

Some private companies, like Colt International Ltd., will carry out a free survey of your premises, checking everything from heating and lighting to ventilation — and even noise!

In your own survey, be satisfied that the space available can be used effectively and is enough for moderate expansion. If business booms, you don't want to be involved in moving in the early stages.

If you are building your own premises, choose the right type of architect carefully. Some specialise in industrial buildings; the Royal Institute of British Architects will assist you in your choice.

Instant accommodation is possible through the wide variations of prefabricated buildings now available, such as the 'Portakabin'.

The units vary in size from about 85 up to 750 sq. ft., and precise fittings, including lighting and equipment, can be tailor-made to meet your individual needs. The units can be interlinked or stacked on top of each other, providing a great degree of flexibility.

Security of your premises cannot be overlooked in these days of thieves and vandals. The main sources of theft, however, are customers, staff and visitors, and individual services to detect and deter these are provided by the increasing number of private security firms, such as Group 4.

These include night watchmen, personnel identity and searching, transit of cash and valuables, and bonded stores.

Be aware of fire risks and make sure your equipment is up-to-date and that staff know how to use it; regular fire drills are common-sense.

Communications

Keeping in touch with your customers could be the life-blood of your new business. Most consumers value easy and direct access to suppliers and for this reason it is important for you to weigh up the communication angles before you start.

If you are to be involved with delivery of goods, or if your service has to be taken to the client, the most appropriate transport medium should be selected.

Are the road networks adequate or could better coverage be obtained by making use of local or national rail services?

Canals can prove quite suitable for some items, such as heavy engineering goods, although naturally the time factor has to be considered. Similarly, although carriage by air is speedy, it can be quite expensive and costs could eat into your profit margin.

Buy a large-scale map of the area you intend to cover and study the viability of the alternative transport facilities available.

Get your products from point of manufacture to point of sale by the quickest and most economical route, which may not necessarily be the shortest. Longer motorway travel, for example, may beat more direct but less major roads.

Whether you run your own delivery vehicles or sub-contract remains a vexed question and choice can be a difficult one. Although contractors' charges may look high, these can only be truly compared with your own running costs where you fully allow for such items as depreciation and management time. The alternatives to which you could put your own capital should also be considered.

Competitive carrying facilities are offered by several private concerns, whilst the Post Office puts on display a host of specialised services for the businessman, as follows:

Direct Bag Service: for senders of regular quantities to a single address Cash on Delivery Service.
County Parcels: Reduced rates for distribution within a defined area, usually a group of counties.
Nightrider: Fast, overnight delivery of parcels up to 22.5 kg.
Datapost: Courier delivery of important packages.
Expresspost: Same day, messenger collection and delivery service.
Air Parcels Service: For exports.

The Post Office also offers a bulk rebate service, freepost and/or business reply, and discounts on sending second-class mail. Ask at any Post Office for their literature.

If you do go in for your own vehicles, ensure that what you buy is the right shape as well as the right size for what you are carrying. Does a high tailgate mean longer — and therefore more expensive — loading?

Is the vehicle going to be reliable, or are costly breakdowns likely to cause chaos? What sort of warranty does the manufacturer or supplier provide? Are spare parts readily available?

A major decision will be whether to buy, hire purchase or lease. Capital considerations you can probably decide for yourself but discuss taxation differences with your accountant. Don't be misled by rather extravagant claims for the benefits of leasing advertised by the less reputable companies engaged in this field. See Chapter 11 for further details.

Be ready with a communication alternative and have your plans laid *before* an emergency occurs.

Plant and Machinery

Most businesses, however small, need to acquire some assets under this heading. It is well worth it in the long run to give a great deal of thought and care to such purchases.

A retailer may rue the day he bought a second-hand refrigerator which turns out to be both unreliable and too small. Equally, a lathe that looked like a bargain at the time is of little use if spares cannot be obtained or if it proves unadaptable to changing methods.

Cost will play a big part in the initial choice and, as with vehicles, leasing and hire purchase should be considered.

If you are setting up in an Area of Expansion, as described earlier in this chapter, grants are available towards the cost of new machinery or plant on premises used for qualifying activities. These can be paid to the purchaser or, in the case of hired assets, to the owner.

Plan carefully before any fixed asset is given its final resting place. Is the floor in that area suitable and will it bear the load? Are main facilities within easy reach, or are repiping and mains servicing going to add to installation costs?

More importantly as far as positioning is concerned, ensure proper siting for the most economical work-flow. Many small industrialists fail to appreciate how costly their badly placed machinery can be.

Frustrating delays or additional footwork, through lack of fore-thought, can have an adverse effect on your workers. Be ready to consult them before siting decisions are finalised; being closer to the job than you are makes their contribution worthwhile.

Machinery needs to be delicately handled and it can pay dividends to employ a specialist removal firm when heavy items are installed or moved.

Once in place, careful handling does not end there and employees must be trained in the proper use of their machinery. This again will save money later, for improper handling is bound to result in costly repair bills — and perhaps an accident.

Regular maintenance is essential and the more complex the plant, the more thought is required. Have contingency plans been laid to allow for breakdowns? Do you know how long it takes to rush spare parts to the scene? Is a reliable after-sales service available?

Keep a check on your own technology to keep abreast — or ahead — of your competitors. Trade journals will have news of the latest processes or more revolutionary machinery. Business can be lost overnight to someone else able to provide a more rapid turnover or a higher quality article at the same unit cost.

Be one step ahead, also, of the factory inspector. His regular visits should result in complimentary back-slapping and not instructions to fit extra guard rails or relay slippery floor surfaces.

Personnel

It is no coincidence that labour takes the largest proportion of turnover in most businesses. It really is the most important factor.

Whilst a Government department or a monopoly trader can survive despite occasionally insolent service, no private concern can last for long, or indeed expand, if the labour force is unsuitable. Healthy competition will quickly rectify such a situation and put unhelpful firms out of business.

Always, always employ the best possible staff you can obtain and afford. To save, say, 10p an hour by accepting a lower level of skill, be it secretarial or engineering, will turn out to be a handicap to the business in the longer term.

Friendly, skilful, conscientious staff will build a happy workplace and a successful enterprise will result.

It also follows that if employees are satisfied they will stay put and this continuity of personnel will produce a more efficient business.

Recruiting sources may be advertisements in newspapers or trade magazines, staff agencies or the Government's Employment Service Agency. Whilst word-of-mouth can be employed, one of these major sources should also be made use of to provide you with a wider choice.

State clearly what the job entails, hours worked, and holidays and fringe benefits, if any. Do *not* promise 'opportunities for promotion' unless these are specific, or you will finish up with frustrated staff continually awaiting upgrading.

Sorting through the many written applications — for this is the best initial method — can be soul-destroying but keep in mind what you require that person to do. If you are seeking a toolfitter, it is not necessary that he be able to compose a businesslike letter. Try and read between the lines to gauge the applicant's approach to the job.

If certain qualifications, whether gained through study or experience, have been requested, the applicant should have confirmed that he has these.

When interviewing, put the applicant at ease and you will discover his more natural self. Explain clearly what is required and make notes of relevant points, especially if several people are to be interviewed. It would be disastrous to later appoint someone other than you thought!

Listen to what he has to say and ask questions that are more likely to produce a detailed answer than just 'Yes' or 'No'. Treat all candidates as potential customers.

Pay will naturally vary from region to region and within different types of employment, but check on Government subsidies where applicable.

In a 'closed shop' industry, trade union procedure must be followed and, if necessary, advice sought from the Advisory, Conciliation and Arbitration Service (A.C.A.S.).

Training of staff is both in your interest and conducive to better relations with customers. Dealing with unqualified staff tends to send your customer in a different direction next time.

On-the-job training needs to be supplemented, in an increasing number of cases, by tuition via industrial training boards, local technical colleges, trade bodies or the Training Service Agency. (See also Chapter 10.)

Cash grants are often available and, in the designated Assisted Areas, instructors can be called upon. These will help train employees in your own workshop or at Government-run skillcentres.

Bear in mind that your organisation may have to operate a half-day or full day when a trainee is away.

Keep the welfare of your staff uppermost in mind and you will be repaid. Always be available to give advice on professional or personal problems.

Accidents do happen at work and it is your legal and moral responsibility to be prepared. An adequate first-aid box must be provided as an absolute minimum, and a study made of the Health and Safety at Work etc., Act for those requirements relevant to your industry or profession (see Chapter 5).

Legal obligations in cases of termination or redundancy exist and the letter of the law must be followed. Written warnings are often obligatory and legal advice should be sought in potentially difficult instances.

Remember that secretarial services can often be obtained on a shared basis through a reliable agency.

Stock

This will vary from cans of beans to ingots of zinc and any advice must obviously be general. However, certain rules and safeguards apply whatever the commodity.

Stock is cash — at least after you have paid for it — and if you treat it with the same care it will repay you just as much as if you had left the money earning interest elsewhere.

You will probably have a choice of suppliers and only experience will tell which offers the most competitive service. Price alone is no comparison. It is no good appointing the cheapest supplier and then finding you are losing production time through delays in delivery.

Make use of more than one stock merchant. This will enable you to compare the services offered and also give you an emergency supply in the event of one failing to deliver the goods.

Careful financial planning is essential to help you decide exactly what goods are needed and when. Perishable items may need to be re-ordered daily. With others, a weekly or monthly order will suffice. Check your requirements to make sure you are not ordering too much. Excess stock on the shelves, be it a shop or a factory, is dead money; only when it is turning over rapidly is it paying for itself.

Seasonal goods must be ordered earlier than others and as the end of season approaches, scale your orders down accordingly. Better to run out at the end of the season than to carry surplus goods forward.

Calculate in what quantities it is preferable to place your orders. Bulk buying may attract larger discounts.

Be certain that you know the terms of trade for payment. If you are expected to pay within 30 days of being invoiced, don't give your business a bad name by taking 60 days. You may discover that your buying has suddenly dried up!

Can you save money by picking up your own requirements instead of having them delivered? If your own delivery vehicle has spare capacity, this is well worth investigating.

Fluctuating commodity prices need daily watching to time your orders correctly. Plumbers, in particular, soon recoup the cost of the *Financial Times* each day by keeping regularly abreast of copper prices.

Maintain proper records and be in a position at any time to know exactly what period present stocks will cover.

If necessary, safeguard your stocks by keeping them under lock and key, with an 'Out and In' book to maintain updated levels.

A neat and tidy system will save time and a numbering method enable you to take quicker checks. Appoint someone, if a full-time storeman is unnecessary, to be responsible for stock held.

Finally, if a waste by-product is being produced in addition to your main line, treat this as a stock item. Look after it, record it, find a market for it and thereby bring down the basic cost of your operation.

Accounting Methods

Most businesses use some form of accounting machinery, from the simple keyboard variety to computer terminals. You are unlikely in the early stages to require anything too sophisticated but whatever your needs a careful and considered choice should be made.

You will be parting with a not inconsiderable portion of your initial capital and it is vital that the machines you choose prove suitable for the medium term needs of the business.

Even the choice of typewriter — you will almost certainly need one — is important. Some customers may be linked with your firm by letter only and a poorly produced document will not do the image any good. You can't *always* blame the typist!

Your accountant is the man to ask before committing yourself to any heavy outlay on accountancy aids. A white elephant you do not want and anything you purchase in order to save manual time must do just that.

Alternatively, see what the market has to offer but remember two things; try any machine before you actually buy and don't be swayed by over-extravagent claims made by commission-earning salesmen.

Do speak to a firm specialising in accounting methods (like Kalamazoo) for, without charge, they will gladly advise you on basic needs.

Your purchase and sales records will probably benefit by mechanisation, especially if the business is expanding rapidly. P.A.Y.E., V.A.T., and other records may also be handled more easily.

There is a wide variety of desk calculators and adding machines available; again, try before you buy. A Post Office franking machine is worth considering if large quantities of mail are going out daily.

Filing is all part of efficient recording and a proper system should be evolved as quickly as possible. Rapid reference to earlier records will save valuable secretarial and managerial time.

With growth, the aid of computers should be considered. The market is like a minefield, however, with about 2/300 companies competing for your business. The most logical approach is to invest in the services of a computer specialist (such as I.C.F.C.) who has no links with any particular manufacturer. The advice may cost you about 10% of the total to be invested in a computer but will be money well spent. Purchases, Sales, Wages, Invoicing, Stocks and Profit and Loss Accounts can all be speedily and efficiently handled by today's computers. (See also Chapter 11.)

No system is any better than those maintaining it and an alert, efficient office staff is your best method of success.

If you have been fortunate enough in employing first-class administrative staff, the accounting side of the business will be one less headache for you to worry about.

Buying an Established Business

Most businesses which change hands as going concerns in the U.K. are shops, although the general rules to follow are much the same in any trade.

Primarily, find out why the present owner wants to sell. Don't accept his word for this but make your own subtle enquiries to establish the true reason. One indicator may be what he intends doing afterwards.

Carry out a thorough survey of the business and if it is a retail outlet, watch at different times on differing days to weigh up the number of customers.

How long has the business been on the market? The original asking price can usually be knocked down, just as in the case of a house sale.

A seasonal business needs careful timing of purchase and it would be unwise, for instance, to miss the Christmas boom in the toy trade or to start ice-cream manufacture in the winter.

If the business is a limited company, and you are acquiring the shares, legal advice must be sought as to what liabilities you are assuming. Check, in any case, whether you will be responsible for current debtors and creditors and also for any other payments due.

Goodwill is almost impossible to define but, looked at widely, it is the hope — and no more — that the existing customers will continue their support for the new owner. You may have to pay for this 'asset' and it will be very dependent on past profits, locality, competition in the area and other factors. Your bank manager should be able to guide you on this point.

If you are relying on local trade, make sure you have a wide knowledge of the area. Walk around and get the 'feel' of the locality. Is it declining or growing? What developments are taking place or being planned? A visit to the Local Authority should provide answers to the last two questions.

At least three years' audited accounts are essential to provide the trends of turnover and profit. Go through the figures with your accountant or banker and adjust them as necessary. If a manager was previously employed but you intend taking on this role yourself, some alteration to the wages figure may be called for.

Overhead costs should be normal for the particular trade and wide variations in these, or in gross or net profit margins, will need careful analysis.

Figures since the last audit will probably be provided but treat them with the care which any unaudited figures demand. Check that suppliers will continue the same terms of trade.

If property is involved, a solicitor should arrange the conveyancing but before contracting, get him to ensure that any leases are to your liking and that no restrictive covenants exist. If the lease is a short one, large rent increases may take place at renewal.

Stock should be readily saleable and not 'stale'. Equipment needs to be reasonably modern and in working order, or replacement costs may put a burden on the business sooner than expected.

If staff are employed, will they continue under your leadership? Specialised personnel, in particular, should be retained if at all possible.

Franchise Operations

Franchising is rapidly becoming one of the fastest growth sectors around the world and in Britain, for instance, by the end of 1984 sales through franchised businesses had almost doubled over a 2-year period.

In return for a sum of money you are given the right to trade under a nationally recognisable name. The franchisor looks after advertising and training, and provides you with his merchandise and, usually, ongoing management advice. You, however, are left to manage.

Famous names using this method include:

Coca Cola	Pro-nuptia wedding clothes
Wimpey Bars	Spud-u-like
Golden Egg	Kentucky Fried Chicken
Arnold Palmer golf ranges	Dyno-Rod
B.S.M. driving schools	Computerland
Prontaprint	Holiday Inns
Spar grocers	

and many others.

Some franchise operations are obviously better run than others and as careful a study should be made of your intended 'partner' as if you were going it alone. The British Franchise Association, set up in 1977 to foster franchising in the U.K., is a useful regulatory body which has nearly 100 member companies. Its advice is well worth seeking.

An offshoot of the industry's success is the number of specialist consultants and, although their services do not come cheaply, an hour or two listening to advice may not come amiss. The major clearing banks also have franchise managers who may be able to help you through one of their branch managers.

The average cost of a franchise is perhaps £30,000 although purchase prices vary from just £5,000 to over £300,000. The typical franchisee tends to be a married man under 40 with two children who has either lost his job or fed up with a 9 to 5 existence. Be prepared to work very long — and unsocial — hours!

Very few franchises fail, partly no doubt because of the size of the proprietor's initial stake but also due to the franchisor's desire to make the venture mutually successful!

Franchising contracts normally last between 7 and 10 years and you should certainly obtain legal advice as to the clauses they contain.

The rewards can be very high but do expect to have to put a lot of effort into the business, especially in the early years.

CHAPTER 5

Taking Professional Advice

Introduction

A common failing amongst many smaller businessmen is their insistence on doing everything themselves.

Not one of them would contemplate making all their own letter deliveries, relying instead on the professionals in the shape of the Post Office.

Similarly, where other professional bodies exist to provide specialist services they should be consulted. It is false economy, and can even lead to contravention of our laws, to rely always upon your own opinion or judgement.

Find yourself a good solicitor and make him earn his bread — and yours! Proper legal advice in business may save you thousands of pounds, or even a spell in jail!

Financially scratch the brains of your bank manager and accountant. And, finally, tell a reliable insurance broker that you expect him to give you 100% coverage and service.

Of course all this will cost you money. But we have already agreed that your philosophy is 'speculate to accumulate', haven't we?

The 'Right' Status

One of your earliest decisions will be whether you are going to run your business as a sole trader or in the form of a partnership or limited company. These are the only three choices available to you in this country.

No particular course is right or wrong, but you should give careful thought to the advantages and disadvantages of each before deciding.

Sole Trader: As a sole trader (or proprietor) you accept full responsibility and liability for the business. In the eyes of the law you and the business are one and, if things go wrong, you cannot, for instance, claim that certain personal assets are distinguishable from any 'owned' by the business. All will go into the pool to pay creditors if bankruptcy catches up with you. You can, of course, employ other people to work for you.

Partnerships: This is a very similar set-up, except that you share either the financing or the running, or both, with someone else. Or there may be a few of you.

If things go wrong, however, the same rules apply and your personal possessions may have to be sold to clear any outstanding debts. You and your partners are liable, incidentally, for *all* of the partnership debts and not just a proportion.

It is advisable to have a Partnership Deed drawn up to sort out matters such as responsibility and distribution of profits. If no Deed is in existence and a dispute arises, the Partnership Act of 1890 steps in and decides the issue for you.

Choosing your partner or partners should be treated with great respect. It is almost like selecting a husband or wife and similar 'requirements' must be considered. Could you 'live' with your prospective partner for the rest of your life? You certainly intend working with him for that period.

Many partnerships blossom and bring forth profitable fruit, others are the scene of constant rowing and disagreement. You can see the similarities with marriage!

If your husband or wife is your business partner as well, this is just as much a legal partnership as any other and the same rules apply. The Act of 1890 defines a partnership as one where 'two or more people (are) working together with a view to profit' and the existence of this is sometimes ignored — until the law steps in!

Limited Companies: This is a rather more complex arrangement although very basically all that it does is to separate the assets and liabilities of the business so that they are distinguishable from your own.

A limited company therefore becomes a legal entity in its own right in the eyes of the law. It can sue, or be sued, independently of its officers, the directors of the company. It can even be given a prison sentence, which the directors would serve on its behalf!

More importantly, its members (i.e. the shareholders) are limited in their personal liability and, if the company goes into liquidation, can lose only the capital (and possibly any loans) they have subscribed.

Various Companies Acts oversee the proper running of both private (the vast majority) and public companies. Annual returns have to be made, including the filing of a Balance Sheet and Profit and Loss Account. These, in turn, can be inspected by any member of the public.

The cost of setting up a limited company can be from £125 upwards.

Whichever type of base you establish for your business may in part be governed, apart from personal preferences, by taxation implications and here you should seek advice from your accountant. There can, in fact, be significant tax advantages if a new business starts as a sole trader or partnership rather than as a company.

Unlike companies, the first year's profits (if any!) of a partnership or individual form the basis of the tax assessment for two or three years. Often the first 12 months' profits will be low, in which case the tax payable in the first two or three years will also be low.

If, in fact, a loss is incurred in a partnership, it may be offset against the partners' other income for the corresponding tax year or the following year. And, as explained in an earlier chapter, where a partnership or sole trader incurs losses during the first few years of business, such losses may be carried back for up to three years and set against the individual's total taxable income for those years. As a result, someone who has given up a salaried employment to set up in business as a sole trader or partnership may be able to recover some or all of the income tax paid on his salary during the final years of his previous employment.

With a company, only its own losses can be set against other income and profits of the company itself.

Whilst it is relatively easy to transfer the business of a partnership to a company, the reverse can prove both complex and costly.

There are four main matters to be dealt with in forming a company, as follows:

Choosing a name
Defining the company's business (known as its 'objects')
Settling its constitution and procedures
Filing particulars with the Registrar of Companies.

The name must be carefully chosen and certain words such as 'Royal' are banned; others, including 'National' and 'International' need special permission.

Probably the best course of action is to purchase a 'clean' company (your solicitor will do this for you), for by this method it will come with an undertaking that it has not traded nor has any liabilities. This is called 'buying off the shelf' and you merely change the name to the one you have chosen by a simple transfer.

A company does not have to trade under its own name but may adopt a different trading name. Care is required, however, to ensure that the name used cannot be confused with anyone else's already in use.

A notice containing the business name and address should be displayed at all business premises to which customers and suppliers have access.

Letterheads must show the address of the registered office, registered number and country of incorporation and the name of the company. If any directors' names are shown, then they must *all* be included.

The Registry of Business Names has now been abolished and it is no longer necessary to register where you are not using your own name. Limited Company names, however, still have to be registered and your accountant or solicitor will deal with this aspect for you.

Never be too flamboyant with your choice of name, for the public is wary of outlandish titles. A company registered as 'Huge Success Ltd.' went into liquidation not long after incorporation owing over £100,000!

Four Just Men

Build around you a quartet of useful mentors: four advisers, each specialists in their own sphere, whom you can tap for information and advice as the need arises.

The choice of each should be carefully made. Don't base your decision on either convenience or friendship factors alone.

In the years ahead, as your business progresses, you may increasingly rely on these advisers. For that reason they must be first class.

Ask colleagues for their experiences. Seek recommendations. Draw up a list of potential advisers and visit each in turn. Plainly state your case and the fact that you are visiting his competitors and, finally, appoint the professional who most impresses you.

You will need one of each of the following:

Bank Manager: He should be brought into the picture about your intended business venture at the same time as it is merely a glint in your own eye.

You will already have formulated a few ideas, of course, but make it clear that you are still at the investigatory stage and wish to seek his general advice. Remember, he will have seen many keen amateurs like you before and his contribution should prove invaluable.

Tell him you are merely throwing around ideas and would welcome his opinion. At this stage you may not yet have identified your financing needs and this should be made clear. Later, of course, you may call back with a specific borrowing proposition (see Chapters 3 and 9).

Accountant: Just as in any other profession, there are accountants and accountants. Some will merely call once a year, tick your books and produce a set of figures which won't mean anything to you.

Others will appreciate that every large firm has to start somewhere and, who knows, in a few years' time you may become that accountant's major client.

He should certainly be qualified and show a positive interest in what you are doing. The Institute of Chartered Accountants or the Association of Certified and Corporate Accountants will gladly send you lists of their members in your locality.

Don't rush into appointing one and don't be afraid of changing later if you are dissatisfied; this advice, of course, applies to all your professional appointments.

All sorts of queries will raise their heads in the first year or so and your accountant's opinion may prove invaluable. Try not to bother him too often, but never hesitate to pick up the telephone if you feel advice is needed.

Whatever you do, never appoint a 'friend of a friend' who 'does your books' in his spare time outside his full-time job. It may save you money in the first year but will almost certainly cost you a lot more later in the lack of professional advice and guidance.

Solicitor: It is better to find a suitable solicitor *before* you need him. Don't hesitate in interviewing one or two until you find the right relationship between you. Seeking legal advice in a hurry may land you with the wrong man.

Some practices specialise in business matters, as opposed to conveyancing, crime, divorce and the other multifarious jobs solicitors do, and if you find one all the better. It may cost you a little more in fees but if you are going to specialise in business, it is better if your advisers are specialists too.

Recommendations of business friends as to solicitors used are worth pursuing but if you would like a complete list of practices within your area write to the Law Society. Or ask your bank manager.

Insurance Broker: Advice in this specialised field can be taken either from a broker or from your clearing bank.

Some brokers operate agencies for a limited number of companies and, although they will not tell you, consequently offer a more restricted service than one who has no special links.

Obtain two or three quotations (and seek advice as to what should be covered — dealt with later) but remember that, as in life generally, you only get what you pay for. The cheapest, therefore, may not be the best for you.

Never deal with an insurance company of which you have not heard. There are enough reliable and well-known concerns around without taking this possible risk.

Keep on the Right Side of the Law

Many small businessmen will tell you that one of their biggest headaches is keeping abreast of the legislation which regularly seems to rain down upon them.

Although in a survey carried out by Opinion Research Centre employers did not rank employment laws all that highly on their list of problems, not one of the 301 firms participating answered a test on their knowledge of these laws completely correctly!

Your solicitor will give you basic advice on your legal duties, although he cannot be expected to have a complete knowledge of all the regulations appertaining to your particular business. He should, however, be able to find the answers for you.

If you intend to grant credit, hire out goods or canvass away from your normal trade premises, you will need to register under the Consumer Credit Act, 1974.

The local Chamber of Commerce may answer specific enquiries, as should your own trade federation.

Local authority bye-laws may apply, as well as Parliamentary statutes and, more latterly, E.E.C. rules and customs. Certain forms may have to be 'prominently displayed' in your office, certainly in the case of a limited company.

If you have a new product or process to patent, specifications must be submitted to the Patent Office. This can be a daunting task and you may find it more practicable to seek the advice of a patent agent. Their Chartered Institute will provide a list of members' names and addresses.

You can conduct your own searches beforehand at the National Reference Library of Science and Invention and a wise move would be to obtain the two free booklets issued by the Patent Office, *Applying for a Patent* and *Patents as a Source of Technical Information*.

Once patented you have the right, of course, to allow others to use your process or manufacture your product under licence for an appropriate fee. Patenting can take several years to complete.

Some products may have to conform to the standards of the British Standards Institution who will give you the necessary advice.

A profitable investment may be membership of the National Federation of the Self-Employed and Small Businesses who boast over 50,000 members in Great Britain including some 50 M.Ps. It operates a free legal protection scheme for members.

The Federation, amongst other aims, seeks to protect small businesses from the increasing volume of legislation and what it calls 'bureaucratic suffocation'. Membership is not expensive and there are over 370 branches throughout the U.K. Equally useful could be membership of the Association of Independent Businesses which represents 30,000 firms. Subscription depends on the number you employ.

Another 'pressure group' for the self-employed is the Forum of Private Business.

Many of these organisations speak as one under the umbrella of the T.U.C. where they constitute the Alliance of Small Business and Professional Associations.

You can insure against falling foul of employment laws by joining an agency such as the Employers' Protection Insurance Services or D.A.S. Legal Insurance. For a small annual premium you will be covered for almost all legal costs and any awards made against your firm at an arbitration tribunal.

Several thousand small businesses already take advantage of such schemes and it is well worth investigating. Legal costs alone of an industrial tribunal can reach £1,000.

The Industrial Society has an information service for small businesses providing practical advice on all employment matters.

Some relevant Acts

There was a spate of employment legislation during the 1970s and the pressure on the small business continues without much relief.

You cannot be a full-time businessman and a legal expert, but certain statutes must be complied with and it will be worth your while to find out which are the most relevant to your company.

The following is by no means a concise list but contains (in chronological order) the more recent of the major trade and employment laws currently in force:

Factories Act, 1961: Relates to the safety and welfare of persons employed in factories.

Offices, Shops and Railway Premises Act, 1963: Covers employed persons in these situations.

Weights and Measures Acts, 1963, 1976 & 1979: Covers, as it implies, correct weights and measures of a whole range of goods.

Redundancy Payments Act 1965: Defines redundancy, calculation of payments, and procedures to be followed.

Trade Descriptions Acts 1968 & 1972: Deals with goods, services, accommodation and facilities provided in the course of trade. Regulates advertisements, labels, signs, posters and verbal descriptions.

Equal Pay Act 1970: Gives women the right to equal treatment when they are employed on work of similar nature to that of men.

Fair Trading Act 1973: Set up the office of Director of Fair Trading to act in the interests of consumers.

Health and Safety at Work, etc. Act 1974: Places a duty on most employers to ensure the safety of their workers and the general public at the employer's premises by maintaining safe plant and organising adequate training and supervision.

Trade Union and Labour Relations Act 1974: This establishes for most employees the right not to be dismissed unfairly and enables an employee who thinks he has been badly treated to seek a remedy at an industrial tribunal.

Consumers Credit Act 1974: Provides for radical reforms of the law concerning credit, including hire purchase, personal items, credit cards and trading checks. You will need a licence if you offer any of these facilities.

Employment Protection Act 1975: This legislation set up the Advisory, Conciliation and Arbitration Service and applies to all employers of labour. It also defines pay statements and guarantees payments for short-time working, and covers rights of pregnant women as well as rules governing redundancies. Between 40,000 and 50,000 cases a year are filed with A.C.A.S.

Sex Descrimination Act 1975: Gives equal rights to both men and women in employment, training, education, in the provision of goods and services, and in the management and disposal of premises. It also set up the Equal Opportunities Commission. The Act does not apply to firms with less than five employees.

Race Relations Act 1976: Protects individuals against race discrimination as job applicants, employees, customers, students, and in property matters.

Unfair Contract Terms Act 1977: Makes ineffective any clause excluding liability for death or injury caused by negligence as well as limiting other exclusion clauses concerning loss or damage to goods or property.

Employment Protection (Consolidation) Act 1978: Brings together the provisions on individual employment rights previously covered by several earlier Acts, all of which remain on the Statute book.

Sale of Goods Act 1979: Laying down that goods must be of merchantable quality.

Employment Acts 1980/82: Relate to Trade Union ballots and compensation.

Competition Act 1980: Controls anti-competitive practices.

Supply of Goods and Services Act 1982: Outlines contract terms for the sale and hire of goods and services.

Trade Union Act 1984: Legislation on secret ballots, trade union membership and political expenditure.

Specific industries are further regulated by special rules, such as the catering trade where both the Food Hygiene (General) Regulations 1970 and the Fire Precautions Act 1971 apply. From 30 July, 1979 all cafes, restaurants and public houses selling food must clearly display their prices, under E.E.C. rules.

Recommended guidelines are often in force in addition to statutes. The clothing industry has the Home Laundering Consultative Council, for instance, which is a party to the international care labelling code for clothing and other items (Kitemark).

Pamphlets on most of the above laws are obtainable from the Dept. of Employment, or in certain cases from either the Equal Opportunities Commission or the Office of Fair Trading.

To keep abreast of the many provisions of the Health and Safety at Work, etc. Act, a monthly journal is published available on subscription from Maclaren Publishers Ltd. Since this Act provides for unlimited fines and jail terms of up to two years for offenders, current knowledge may be said to be of self-interest!

Insurance — what to cover

The range of potential disasters that could happen to you once you are in business on your own seems endless. This is where insurance comes in.

Advice you will certainly need and whilst at this early stage of your development you will be watching the pennies, it is foolhardy to over-economise on insurance cover.

Some of the basic contingencies you will certainly need to guard yourself against will be:

Fire and damage to premises
Theft and damage to contents
Public Liability (and possibly product liability as well)
Employer's liability
Loss of profits (possibly)
Damage to vehicles, including business use of a private car if you are, for example, delivering your own goods.

Most of these are common sense; some are legal obligations upon you as an employer. The Health and Safety at Work, etc. Act, for instance, insists that you safeguard the conditions under which your employees work. Members of the public also become your responsibility when visiting your premises and their potential injury or death must be covered.

Special additional insurances may be necessary for such items as plate glass or chemical substances, or perhaps for professional liability in some cases. Consider, also, insuring your debtors with someone like 'Trade Indemnity Credit Insurance'.

Make certain that loss of cash on the premises includes the value of such things as national insurance and postage stamps.

Loss of profits may be a vital endorsement to your policy and looks after you — with a cash payment — should some factor adversely affect business income for several days, or weeks, before you get things straight again.

A fire may disrupt production, destroy essential records and perhaps lose you customers for a period. All of these problems come under the loss of profits heading or 'consequential loss', as it is sometimes known.

Finally, arrange cover on directors' or partners' lives for the benefit of the business in the event of their early demise. Equally, 'key employees' may be included in such a scheme.

Deal with a first-class company that has its own reputation to maintain, and you won't be kept waiting too long for your money in the event of a claim becoming necessary.

You and Yours

Having joined the self-employed ranks, your personal insurance position will warrant review. No longer is an employer in the background, waiting to pay you a pension.

Discuss your own needs, therefore, with your broker and don't forget your spouse and any children. Family income benefits are not normally very expensive to set up but could be a boom to those left behind in the event of a calamity. Do also cover yourself against accidents.

You should also have a self-employed (or controlling director's) retirement plan, the premiums for which may be debited to the business before striking a taxable profit.

A sizeable fund can be amassed over a period of years, since the income and capital gains are entirely tax-free. At retirement you can elect for a lump sum, a pension or a mix of the two. The pension can also be continued to your spouse if you should die first.

Premiums may be paid monthly or annually and may fluctuate from year to year in accordance with the results of the business. In a good year you may pump in more, in a poor year less. At present, no more than 17½% of your earnings (more, if you were born before 1934) can be set aside for this purpose each year.

Additionally, you should have an ordinary life policy, preferably of the endowment type, i.e. one that pays out after a set amount of years as well as on intervening death. If this is a little too expensive to maintaina initially, take out a convertible 'whole life' policy and convert it when income improves.

Finally, consider the benefits of private health insurance, the premiums for which remain fairly modest. A sizeable discount can be obtained if you operate a group scheme for all or some of your employees, providing there are at least five in the scheme.

CHAPTER 6

Sales and Marketing

Introduction

Without much argument, the element most often ignored in small business plans is marketing. A word coined only a generation ago, it embraces much more than mere selling and encompasses the whole art of turning a product or service into cash.

It starts before any production wheels begin to roll and continues smoothly through to the final sale. Although reappraisals and adjustments will be put into effect throughout the process, for marketing to be successful there has to be an initial plan, a set of objectives. Let us look at them.

Setting the Objectives

Before you get very far at all ask yourself two basic questions. 'What business am I in? And what do I want to achieve?'

Many businesses fail to register success simply because they do not recognise in which market they are operating.

Only when a picture postcard manufacturer appreciated that he was part of the entertainment industry, and not a printer, was he able to see other possibilities and thus profitably expand.

Be certain you know which segment of the market *you* are in. Take an outward look instead of an inward one.

What are your aims? Profit may be a basic one but there are others. Many big firms, for instance, seek a larger market share, a quality market, an increase in sales volume, or exclusion of certain rivals. Profit may — surprisingly — appear well down their initial priority list.

Ask yourself 'What can we sell? How many? Where? How? When? At what price?' The answers may reveal certain limitations and these will have to be considered in the overall plan.

If the market you are in is a small one it will be unrealistic to assume a heavy penetration in the early stages. This, in turn, will have financial implications, resulting perhaps in a different strategy.

Set your objectives for three distinct phases, i.e. short-, medium- and long-term. The lengths of these will vary. In the food industry, for example, long-term may mean two years; car manufacturers would look ahead at least ten years.

Make a detailed list of your company's strengths. These might include precision manufacture, a high degree of design or, in the retail trade, the ability to provide consumer goods of a high standard in double-quick time. Build on these strengths, for within them almost certainly lies the key to future success.

Clients will flock to your door simply because you are different. In some specialised way you will make your mark.

Statistics you will already possess as a tool in setting your aims. These alone will not do. Into the formula must go your own intuition; that special 'feel' which every successful entrepreneur must have.

Don't overlook the 'uncontrollables' discussed in Chapter 2. Under 'Pricing Policies' later you will learn a few more!

Your ideals cannot be complete without a thorough appraisal of the opposition. Study your rivals in depth, learn their strategies, try their products. Remember, you will probably be stealing their customers! Looking only at your own plans is akin to a general ignoring the opposing forces lined up against his troops.

Ensure that your own resources are adequate to meet your objectives. To run out of raw materials as sales peak could prove disastrous. Equally, check production capacity, transport availability, finance and so on.

Now define your objectives. Directing them is the next lesson.

Before you move on, however, take another look at the sights you have set and see if there are alternative ways of reaching them. Keep these alternatives up your sleeve. They may prove to be your salvation when market forces suddenly change the picture! Be ahead of your rivals!

Pricing Policies

Just as your personal aims will help to mould your strategy, pricing policies are adjustable with what you have in mind.

Maximising profit may be your underlying ideal but there can be different ways of achieving this. Many large corporations direct that a certain return on capital employed be maintained, whatever profit margin might result. Some are quite prepared to shave margins to the bone to keep out the competition, whilst others aim to maintain a set share of the market at almost any cost. Remember that the multinationals can often afford temporarily to lose money on one product whilst subsidising their costs from profit made on others.

In the early days you may be content merely to match the prices of your competitors, although this policy cannot last if you are to succeed. A much greater degree of sophistication is essential!

Equally, charging 'what the market will bear' can be only a short-term policy. Your aim should be to *create* a market, and the 'right' price to achieve this must be calculated.

In determining this right price, it may well result in a more than adequate profit margin. Consumer goods, in particular, can sometimes be too cheap to attract the right purchaser. Top of the range cosmetics, and certainly many deodorants, are pitched at a high price level on grounds of snobbery or self-satisfaction.

What is your speciality worth to the consumer? If he considers it in the £4 range, then a price of £3 may be just as wrong as £5. How often have you heard 'That's cheap; there must be something wrong with it'?

Cost is only one factor in determining price. Demand — and supply — are others, as are such allied subjects as the terms of trade you offer and any discounts which you may agree to give.

Transportation will affect cost, as will promotion, research and other expenditure. All these varied elements must be built into your costing structure. Naturally, a worthwhile profit must be achievable, but even this factor can have tremendous variations. One man may be content with a 5% return; another larger concern may need to return 8% to allow for capital expenditure.

Most items will have a four-part life cycle and margins may differ in each segment. At the introductory stage investment and promotion costs will be high with low returns, a growth period should then ensue, resulting in a peak of sales which attracts competitors. Finally there is a decline as new products take their place, restarting the cycle.

The uncontrollables are still in evidence in shaping your policy and include the availability of substitutes, the consumer's inherent belief in an 'acceptable' price, and the effect which the market leaders can have if they decide to gang up on you.

'Acceptable' prices, especially amongst the more common food-stuffs, are becoming increasingly noticeable. Ask any housewife what she would 'expect' to pay for butter and you will see what I mean.

If you are dealing in more than one line, be certain what the contribution to profit from each amounts to. This information will help you to decide which lines should be pushed or which dropped entirely.

Don't be surprised if you spot the '80/20 Rule' (Pareto's Law) operating. This has several applications but here may reveal that 20% of your products are providing 80% of profits.

Estimate the overall probability of demand for your units at differing price levels. Establish a price, ensure profitability is still feasible, and be ready to take the next step.

If you feel that you can safely plump for a price enabling some later manoeuvreability, this will help. Staying at the same price level, for instance, but mixing the cost ingredients, could prove an ace up your sleeve if sales begin to fall.

Know Your Consumer

Whether you are in the consumer field or not, someone, somewhere is going to buy your product or service. You should aim to know him better than he knows himself.

Build up a profile of your ideal customer — sex, age, social class, temperament, interests, married state, locality, etc.

Why does he buy your goods? Is it on impulse or after deliberation? When does he buy them? On holiday or at home? During the day or in the evening? Most importantly, how do you let him know you are there? (See 'Advertising' later.)

Specialised firms offer such research, although it can be expensive. The Market Research Society will put you in touch with appropriate member firms, some of which specialise in industrial products.

Statistics available from H.M.S.O. (See Chapter 2) will help and often you will find friends willing to undertake research for you. Field surveys, however, should properly be professionally handled in order to avoid misleading answers.

Patterns of consumer behaviour need to be studied. Wallpaper sales, for example, skyrocket in the weeks before Christmas for the same sort of reason that people buy new toothbrushes before they go off on holiday.

Get to know your customer's whims, his preferences and the reasons for his decisions. Some major marketing agencies will claim, with some justification, that they influence this decision making and that the consumer is a mere toy in their hands. Toys, however, easily break if badly handled.

Define your ultimate customer, find out where he works, lives and plays, and mould what you have to offer in such a way that he cannot refuse.

Moulding Your Product

Merely producing what you have is not enough. It has to be 'shaped' in such a way as to attract the eye — and the pocket — of your ideal client.

Don't be misled by tradition. A pencil may not always prove to be slim and long. Stockings became tights, potatoes 'Smash', quills 'Biros' and the wireless a portable transistor radio, and later still an enclosed printed circuit.

Check size, colour, quality, shape, design and appearance. Can they be improved?'

Is the name right? There should be no confusion, no unpleasant associations. Ford Cars, after much research, still had to change an intended model name after learning to their horror that the word chosen meant something rude in Greek!

What distinctions have you to offer? Does the consumer know? Are there uses other than the intended one?

Ground rules are few in product design although naturally yours should not be inferior to the competition, unless you are aiming down-market.

What satisfaction does the consumer achieve when he buys your product? Have you considered his wishes? Would you attract him more easily if you made your unit more round, more square — or added knobs?

Goods are not always bought for their inherent qualities. Asparagus tips grace dinner tables more for their exclusiveness than their nutrition.

Shelf-life should not be forgotten nor, with slower selling items, possible deterioration — in appearance if not in content. Your products should remain as fresh as when first manufactured.

By now, you have a good picture of the market you are aiming at and should soon be ready with a product or service especially for that market. How are the two going to physically meet?

Distribution

As a retailer this point may not unduly concern you, unless you aim to deliver some of your goods. But as a manufacturer a good distribution network is vital to the successful flow of products from creator to consumer.

The first consideration must be the selection of the right channel.

Ask yourself such questions as 'Where are my buyers? What size will the average order be? Is there an export market?'

These — and several other factors — have to be carefully considered to ensure that from the word go the correct method of transportation is used. Economy will weigh heavily upon your decision but consider also

The size, weight and fragility of the product;

The geographical distribution of your potential market;
The speed of conveyance necessary;
Traditional methods of transportation in your trade; and
Storage problems, if any.

Stock control is an important feature here. Valuable sales could be lost if goods required quickly in the north are being unnecessarily warehoused in the south.

Delivery problems you can do without — there will be plenty of others! So make sure that, whatever method you use, it is speedy, reliable and its cost properly embodied in the prices you charge. And have an alternative up your sleeve!

The Power of Promotion

That promoting a product or a service helps to sell it is without question. What has to be determined is how to promote it, when and where, and what cost should be apportioned under this heading.

Many major companies today will spend as much as 40% of the cost of an item on promoting it. You may say 'What a waste', but of course if the item had not been boastfully brought to the public's attention, then it probably would not have sold at all! You are unlikely to ask for something of which you have never heard.

You should already be aware of the special qualities which you have to offer, having taken a critical look at your product. Now the public at large — or a sector of it — must be told.

Don't be disheartened if you feel you have nothing special to offer; create something. Before the mass market in vodka sales took off only a few years ago, think what the manufacturers had to begin with.

They were trying to sell a colourless, tasteless liquid which did no more for man's bonhomie than any other spirit. Yet out of this they created the typical vodka drinker, put him (and her) in tempting advertisement surroundings and set off what is now a multi-million pound market.

If you are manufacturing and feel that you have designed something particularly appealing, apply to the Design Centre for recognition. Some 12,000 different items have been awarded their distinctive label and this factor can, of course, be used to advantage in your advertising.

The Centre looks for products which are 'satisfactory in terms of performance, safety, construction, ease of use, aesthetics and value for money'.

Timing your promotion is naturally important and such statistics as the fact that some 15% of the population is on holiday during August and not regularly reading newspapers cannot be overlooked.

Make a detailed list of all your potential customers if you are selling to other concerns rather than the consumer. Directories should be utilised, as well as any trade sources to make your list as comprehensive as possible.

Advertising

This will be your best form of communication but where to advertise, when, for how long and how frequently?

Decide firstly at whom you are aiming. Fish fingers are not advertised during peak children's viewing time for fun; the manufacturers know that, whilst mother may buy, the influence comes from the youngsters.

The type of reader of newspaper or magazine chosen is far more important than circulation figures. The fact that 150,000 women read such-and-such a magazine is unlikely to boost your screwdriver sales!

This highlights one of the golden rules to remember about advertising. It does not sell; it only stimulates. Your 'copy' should, initially, attract attention and then retain the reader's or viewer's interest and, finally, persuade him to invest in what you have put before him.

Advertising agencies specialise in this field but their services may not be cheap and, at first, it may be uneconomical to use them. Later, perhaps, the Institute of Practitioners in Advertising can be consulted, and they will put you in touch with some of their 600 member firms.

The importance of timing and frequency of advertising has already been stressed. Anticipated sales at certain price levels will already have been calculated and stock control is thus essential to meet the hoped-for demand. There is little point in planning an advertising campaign to produce a certain level of business unless you are satisfied that you can cope.

A little business in Oxfordshire that had contentedly ambled along for years was suddenly swamped with orders following only one insertion in a national magazine and subsequently went into liquidation as its administration and production were unable to cope with the upsurge in demand.

When using the printed word, try if you can to devise a method of measuring its effect. If coupons have to be cut out and sent to you, for instance, code them so that you know from which newspaper or magazine they come. Similarly, enquire of all telephoned orders how your business came to their attention.

The types of media available for promoting your items go far beyond periodicals and include television, local radio, cinemas, hoardings, exhibitions, and the use of handbills. Exhibiting at trade shows has the additional advantage of weighing up the competition!

Other forms of advertising include using the telephone directory, or issuing clients with 'reminders' such as personalised calenders, desk diaries or pens.

If you have something innovative to offer, issue a Press release to appropriate magazines and you may find such editorial material being used to your advantage without any cost!

Remember, also, if applicable, the value of point-of-sale advertising. Talk shopkeepers into displaying your products in special containers with an appealing, advertising strip to catch the customer's eye.

Whatever copy you produce for your advertisements, bear in mind the strictures of the Advertising Standards Authority, the public's watch-dog, to ensure that what is said is 'decent, legal and honest'. Never make extravagant claims. If the Authority doesn't catch you out, the customer will.

You are, of course, 'advertising' your business in many shapes and forms and such items as your own premises, plant and machinery and vehicles should also reflect your image. Before such giants as Marks and Spencer's buy from a new manufacturer, their inspectors will go over the premises with a fine toothcomb. The background will be as important to them as the goods.

If you have a window of your own, link this with your advertising. Never overfill a window or its clutter may be completely ignored.

Price tickets should be simple, with letters and figures easily readable from a distance. Special offers need to be highlighted and in these cases see if you can obtain financial assistance from the manufacturers involved.

Finally, after deciding how much of your budget you are prepared to allocate towards advertising, find out what 'space' that will buy. If you are convinced that such an investment will prove effective, decide on the best media available, when the most impact will be felt and how regularly it should be maintained.

Packaging

If your goods go into packets, the design of these must be allied with your advertising.

Remember that, with many items, the consumer never sees the actual product at the time of sale. With such things as soup, baked beans, biscuits and pet foods, it is the container which does the initial selling.

It must, therefore, be distinctive and have an immediate appeal for what is inside. It must keep your product in good condition, both in storage and carriage.

If necessary, it must be functional. Consumers are quite prepared to pay a little extra, for example, for shampoos produced in bottles although sachets would be cheaper. Bottles are less messy in use and it is easier to unscrew a cap than run around seeking the scissors!

Beware of any regulations which may apply to the method of packing. And, if you are in the food business, bear in mind that Britain has to conform to the E.E.C.'s labelling directives.

Printing

Let your image come home to the client in everything he sees in print. This will range from your advertisements through letterheadings, catalogues, brochures, visiting cards, photographs and, indeed, any sales literature which you produce.

Make full use of your own delivery vehicles, if owned, for this amounts to eight hours a day, mobile free advertising!

Adopt a 'logo', i.e. a symbol by which your business becomes immediately obvious. Market leaders such as Lloyds Bank and Tube Investments have shown the value of such an approach, which is becoming increasingly popular.

There is no reason why you should not be able to design your own, but if assistance is needed, any public relations or advertising firm will gladly assist for a fee.

The Value of Test Marketing

There is no reason to believe that, simply because you are a small businessman, testing the market with your products is not appropriate. Whilst most major companies try out their new ideas before launching into mass-scale production, you can do the same thing.

It will have to be an expense that you must be ready to write off in the event of failure. But better to lose £500 on a well-researched local campaign than £5,000 on a national launch.

Be ready for disappointment if you are already marketing a number of items and wish to test something new. In the U.S.A., 24 out of 25 tested articles never see more than the first light of day. Similarly, tastes and fashions are ever-changing and one large food concern in this country expects to have only 8% of its products still on sale twelve months later.

Ask selected potential customers to try out your idea for a month. Have a revealing analysis form ready for completion after that period. Adapt where necessary.

Alternatively, test market in the normal way but in a selected area.

Monitor responses and sales. Find out what people think. What improvements would they like to see?

Your enthusiasm may be running away with you in the early stages and test marketing may seem a frustration. But consider its merits; it may be the wisest investment you will make.

Go Out and Sell

Now you're ready for action. Your objectives are set, your product (or service) moulded to suit the consumer you have in mind, and promotion is underway. All you have to do is sell!

Sell not only your product but, more importantly, yourself. Mention any small firm to its clients and the picture conjured up is the man at the helm.

It is *he* who knows their requirements, meets their demands and solves their problems.

So never overlook the vital role you will be playing in promoting your business. When dealing with suppliers, customers or staff, your image must constantly be one of alertness and efficiency. Persuade them to have faith in you and, with that little bit of admitted luck, they might even part with their money!

Consider all aspects of selling, including mail order, direct mail, agencies, the telephone and (where appropriate) vending machines.

Direct mail, carefully choosing the right letterboxes, may on average, with a successful idea, bring a positive response of only 2%. So be ready for heavy mailing costs. Specialist firms will provide you with suitable addresses.

Mail order, via the giants in the field, involves predetermined resources and capacity and should only be tackled after very careful consideration.

It is a growing medium, however, and everything from backscratchers to garden sheds can be sold in this way by both small concerns and giant ones. Any reputable publisher will research your organisation prior to acceptance and you will probably have to show an already proven record in business.

A Sales Force?

You may not yet be ready for an employed sales force but when you are, recruitment must be of the right kind. Most salesmen tend to be extroverts, obviously good conversationalists but not necessarily technically minded.

Unless your idea, therefore, is a particularly technological one, the man or woman you should seek is one with more plus points for personality than for an over-enquiring mind. Let them be salesmen first and technicians second.

Add up their real cost before becoming over committed. To the salary should be added your National Insurance contributions, commissions, expenses, car provision costs and any other 'perks' provided. What will you do when they are on holiday?

Reward should be allied to performance but not at the expense of your set objectives. To merely pay commission for increasing sales may clash with your plans for gradual growth and, indeed, play havoc with your cash flow.

Calculate how long your sales force is able to spend on actual selling as opposed to travelling, waiting for clients, or filling in forms.

Measure salesmen's results carefully and, if appropriate, let them follow through their own orders. This helps to eliminate departmental blame for delays and, as a bonus, highlights problems that might otherwise have gone unnoticed.

Ensure communication is good between customer, salesman and the production team, and install a two-way reporting system to give you a balanced view.

Finally, train and supervise your salesmen to the degree that their own competence instils in them a feeling of team work. The benefits to their pockets will then be matched by a corresponding increase in your own bank balance!

CHAPTER 7

Exporting

Introduction

'Not for me', did you say? If you thought exporting was only for the big boys, like Courtaulds and I.C.I., you could not be further from the truth.

Thousands of very small businesses in the United Kingdom have a foothold in foreign markets. Many had never considered the possibility of exporting until prompted or encouraged by self-employed colleagues or perhaps by their Chamber of Commerce.

The vast range of goods (and services) sold overseas is as wide as those obtainable on the home market. Cars we all know about. Engineering parts are shipped by the thousand. But sand? Yes, millions of tons are dredged from our southern shores and shipped regularly to building sites across the hemisphere.

No state is self-sufficient and one country usually has more of one thing than another — or can make it more cheaply or of better quality. Barter, but with cash interposing, will never die.

Don't let distance put you off. Our second largest buyer is the U.S.A. And if we look at imports into France, America accounts for 7% of their total whilst Britain's share is only 5% — and consider the difference in mileage between!

The export market is not an easy one, but once conquered can be extremely profitable. Problems without doubt exist, and claiming your money back from some, say, eight thousand miles away is no easy matter. But build an element of unpredictability into your export budget and the chances are you will make a success of it. First explore your market . . .

Market Research

You must be prepared to look closely into the available possibilities before getting your feet wet.

You already know what you produce and have an idea as to your ideal consumer. There is no reason to believe that he shouldn't live in Holland as much as here in the U.K.!

Who can help you find him? Some of the sources are:

British Overseas Trade Board;
Chambers of Commerce;
Institute of Export;
Overseas Departments of the Clearing Banks.

Useful publications include:

Trade and Industry (weekly from H.M.S.O.)
Hints to Businessmen (series of booklets on individual countries from the Dept. of Trade)
Europe: a Checklist (from H.M.S.O.)
Technical Help to Exporters (British Standards Institution)
Services for British Exporters (British Overseas Trade Board)
Worldwide Export Publicity (Central Office of Information)
How to Start Exporting (Small Firms Information Service)

The Department of Trade operates an Export Services and Promotions Division providing a quick assessment of the potential overseas market for any particular product. It will also tell you what competition to expect, customs and import regulations and any local tastes or preferences likely to affect your product. The Department is especially helpful to new firms.

The British Overseas Trade Board (B.O.T.B.) offers a wide range of assistance to companies selling overseas, whether they are doing so for the first time or have years of experience behind them. The B.O.T.B. can help with market advice, with specific information about export opportunities, and with practical and financial help in entering new overseas markets. This includes support for exhibiting abroad, for overseas market research, and for travelling to and setting up sales facilities in markets abroad. Particular services are as follows:

The BOTB's *Market Branches* in London can provide basic market information about everything from tariffs to local marketing methods and the economic and commercial climate. They keep in close touch with commercial staff in diplomatic Posts abroad. They are in the same building as the Statistics and Market Intelligence Library where companies may do their own research on facts and figures.

The Export Representative Service will help firms to find an overseas agent in the market they wish to enter.

The Market Prospects Service will give you an assessment of the prospects for your product or service in a particular market as well as helping you to find an agent.

The Overseas Status Report Service provides a check on the capability and general standing (not financial) of a prospective partner.

Technical Help to Exporters will identify overseas standards and technical requirements and advise you how to meet them.

The Export Marketing Research Scheme provides attractive financial support for overseas market research.

The Export Intelligence Service can provide details of export opportunities for a particular product or service as soon as they are reported from abroad.

Generous financial and technical support is available for exporters at trade fairs and exhibitions abroad.

The Outward Mission Scheme provides travel agents to exporters who visit the market in an organised mission.

The Market Entry Guarantee Scheme will provide 50% towards the cost of setting up sales facilities in overseas markets. This contribution is repayable by a levy on sales: if there are no sales no repayment is required. Minimum funding is £20,000.

The B.O.T.B. Publicity Unit can advise on the promotion of products in overseas markets.

The Simplification of International Trade Procedures Board (S.I.T.P.R.O.) can provide information about export documentation and procedures.

The Overseas Projects Fund can be a source of assistance for companies pursuing major capital projects overseas, if it is likely to increase significantly their chances of winning the contract.

All businesses are eligible for these services and any of the Board's regional offices may be contacted.

Currently running is a campaign to encourage more small businesses to become exporters and the Board is offering an introductory voucher worth £150 to any firm which has so far not used its services. The voucher can be offset against the charge for, for example, a market report or stand at an overseas exhibition.

Your clearing bank will be able to guide you on trading conditions abroad, opportunities which may exist and other countries' exchange control regulations, as well as helping with financing and ways and means of receiving payment. Foreign contacts can also be made through this source.

Some of the banks maintain updated booklets on countries abroad and Lloyds Bank, for instance, publishes over 100 such titles.

Libraries are another fruitful source of information and the larger ones stock useful directories. A comprehensive list of these is contained in the Small Firms Information Service brochure *Seeking*

Company Information (International and Foreign Sources). The Department of Trade operates a comprehensive library in London, known as the Statistics and Market Intelligence Library.

The use of all these sources of information can, of course, only guide you through the exporting jungle. It is up to you to find a clearing. Issues to consider should include the following:

(1) The size of any market to be explored;
(2) The political and economic stability of that country;
(3) Growth patterns, as evidenced by recent statistics, and your own view as to the potential;
(4) Habits of the local populace;
(5) Competition — from exporters and from local industry;
(6) Available distribution networks;
(7) Legal and customs regulations, including licence needs.
(8) Standard of quality expected by potential purchasers.

Ensure, naturally, that your productive capacity will meet the requirements of your sales plan. And that deliveries will, as far as can be envisaged, be made on time. Enquire about the Post Office's Argonaut Services.

Set the price 'right' and build in some allowance for disruption, finally adding a 'bargaining margin'. Foreign importers, especially agents, often feel they have to knock you down on price to justify the deal.

Make sure your international bookwork can cope with strange forms and perhaps differing methods of payment. Set up a system of quick liaison with your buyer; a G.P.O. telex machine could prove a wise investment.

Promoting your Product

After the bookwork comes the hard work. Depending upon the type of product or service, differing methods of promotion and selling may apply. There are four basic channels:

(1) Selling direct to an importer;
(2) Selling to a U.K. buying house for foreign firms;
(3) Using an Export House with its own overseas selling organisation; or
(4) Dealing through an agent abroad.

The choice is yours although it is not difficult to see, for instance, that greater risks may be inherent in using an agent as opposed to an

Export House, where payment is made in this country on normal credit terms. But of course these services have to be paid for and your profit margin may be slimmed.

A recent survey of 43 companies selling abroad found a strong connection between the methods used and the level of success achieved. The best results generally went to those which progressed step by step (direct exports, then an agent abroad, followed by an overseas sales subsidiary and finally a production subsidiary) because of the expertise gained at each step.

Particular care must be exercised over your choice of agent; the Courts are kept busy with wrangles between disgruntled agents and frustrated exporters!

Your research may have provided you with potential agencies; advertising abroad should produce further possibilities. Check every reference offered — and a few more! A good bank response is essential and any agent worth his salt will have no difficulty in providing one.

See how thoroughly your prospective agent appears to know his market. Does he speak English? Lack of this may make communication difficult. Is he acting for similar British concerns and, if so, how will he divide his loyalties?

Once you are satisfied, have your solicitor draw up terms of agreement. They should include details of geographical areas to be covered, commissions and expenditure payable and, just in case, methods of arbitration.

Export houses will relieve you of nearly all documentation and may well initially prove the best method of entry into foreign markets for the small business. The British Export Houses Association will provide you with a list of their members. As you grow, you may then wish to take on further tasks yourself.

Marketing in a foreign country requires special expertise and great care has to be exercised to ensure that your product will be fully acceptable.

Packaging may need revising, and health and technical requirements will warrant study. Customs practices — as well as regulations — vary from country to country, but diligent research should provide the answers.

Your chosen colour for both product and package may need revising. White goods, for instance, are difficult to sell in areas of the East, for this colour signifies mourning.

Finally, don't expect to do all your selling from your desk. Importers being regularly visited by your Continental or Japanese competitors will also expect to see you occasionally. Such visits must, of course, be carefully planned, and travelling costs built into your estimates.

If you are successful, consider applying for the Queen's Award for

Export Achievement, entitling you to display the emblem on stationery, packaging and products to the potential benefit of the company.

Documentation

As we have seen, the majority of the paperwork involved with exporting can be avoided if you make use of an Exporting House. A forwarding agent will also look after it for you; names can be obtained from the Institute of Freight Forwarders.

It is advisable, however, to have some knowledge of the necessary documentation, if only to give you a clearer understanding of what is involved.

Staff can be sent on short courses such as the one on Export Documentation run by the Manpower Services Commission. Alternatively, you may wish to recruit someone with the Institute of Export's examination or send an employee on a Foundation Course on Overseas Trade run by the British Overseas Trade Board at some 30 colleges.

Good reference books are available, two of the leading ones being *Croner's Reference Book for Exporters* and *Benn's Exporters Year Book (Export Data)*.

Certificates of origin, invariably required, can be provided by your Chamber of Commerce.

Bills of Lading are perhaps the most common forms in use. These are merely receipts issued by shipping companies after goods have been loaded on board. They are documents of title and must be forwarded to the buyer, or an agent, so that he may claim the goods on arrival in a foreign port.

Goods carried by air are similarly covered by Air Waybills although these are not title documents.

It is important to know what details your invoice should show in addition to normal descriptions. Weight may need to be stated, for example, or construction details of packing cases.

If you are selling direct, the exporting procedure will be along the following lines, with amendments or additions varying according to the country of destination.

Is an export licence required?
Register goods for freight;
Pre-enter at Customs, if necessary;
Prepare invoice and Certificate of Origin;
Lodge Bill of Lading,
Insure
Enter at Customs.

How Will You Get Paid?

Getting your money is the most rewarding part of the exercise. But even this has to be planned.

International methods of reimbursement vary from the procedures you are familiar with at home, and may include one of the following:

Documentary Letter of Credit:

The buyer will arrange with a British bank for you to receive payment upon presentation of certain documents, as clearly defined in the Letter of Credit. These may be revocable or irrevocable.

The bank concerned will check your documents very carefully. Certain international rules exist for this kind of paperwork and these can be found in 'Uniform Rules for Collections' obtainable from your Chamber of Commerce.

Bill of Exchange

Like a cheque in reverse, this is a demand for payment of a specific sum of money on a specified date. The buyer will usually 'accept' the Bill (by signing it) and thus bind himself to pay. The bill may be payable immediately ('at sight') or perhaps after 30, 60 or 90 days.

Naturally, the value of an accepted Bill very much depends upon the standing of the importer.

Payment Against Documents

Here the importer agrees to pay when the documents to title are in his hands.

Open Account

This equates to the usual method of home payment, although funds are more likely to be despatched in the form of a cable or air mail transfer, or perhaps a draft, rather than a cheque.

Any payments agreed must, of course, state whether freight charges and/or insurance are included. Commonly used terms include:

C & F: Cost and freight to a specified destination; insurance not included.
C.i.f.:   Cost, insurance and freight, again to a specified port or town.
F.o.b.:   Free on board. The cost, including delivery of the goods aboard a named vessel.
F.a.s.:   Free alongside ship. The cost, including delivery of the goods to a named quayside.

You may find that, instead of your quoting in sterling, importers will prefer to know the price in local currency. Whilst a straightforward conversion should not present any problem, by the time you receive your money (to be converted into sterling) exchange rates may have gone against you. Although, equally, they may turn in your favour, this is not the sort of trading gamble which you should be taking.

Invoicing in sterling isolates you from exchange risks and makes your goods appear cheaper if sterling is weak. Against these advantages, however, is the fact that if sterling strengthens, your prices start to look expensive. Additionally, the importer is never very sure of *his* selling prices, assuming the items are being on-sold.

If you elect to receive a foreign currency, the answer is to 'cover yourself forward'. If you expect to receive, say 2,000 DM by a set date, you may sell these forward to your bank at an agreed — and fixed — rate of exchange. Supply and demand for the currency in which you are dealing will decide whether that rate is at a premium or a discount against the day's 'spot' rate for immediate transactions.

Any premium payable should be treated as a type of insurance payment.

Such forward cover does involve a liability on your part since if the DMs are received late (or not at all!) you still have to meet your contract with the bank, if necessary by buying at the spot rate to sell the currency back again. Some flexibility in the anticipated receipt date can, however, be arranged.

Bridging the Finance Gap

Expect longer settlement terms in some cases than the one, two or three months you are used to in the U.K. Three to six months credit requirements are not unusual, especially in the Middle East.

How do you finance production for such long periods? Naturally your credit worthiness will be influenced by many factors, not least of all by the time you have been in business.

Even for newcomers, however, finance can be arranged. There are varied sources but the place to start is your clearing bank.

If Bills of Exchange are the means of effecting eventual payment, the Bills themselves may be acceptable as security for bank borrowing. Alternatively, they may be discounted, i.e. sold for something less than their face value. The discount thus charged is the return to the lender, who will collect the proceeds of the Bill when it falls due for payment.

Although the Government does not itself provide finance for exporters, it operates, through its Export Credits Guarantee Department, insurance cover (see below) which in turn can be used to obtain bridging finance.

The policy may be accepted by a bank as collateral, either informally or by means of an assignment of the rights. Some banks operate a 'Smaller Exporters' Scheme' covered by the bank's own E.C.G.D. policy.

E.C.G.D. may also agree, in suitable cases, to issue a guarantee in favour of your bankers. This will entitle you to borrow up to 100% of the value of the transactions at a fine interest rating, currently 5/8% over the bank's base rate.

A revolving limit is normally agreed, reviewed on an annual basis.

One final method of financing worth looking into is forfaiting, similar to E.C.G.D. backing but handled by bankers rather than a Government department. More importantly, the financier forfeits the right of recourse to the exporter.

Insurance

This can be organised by yourself or left to a shipping agent, broker or your bank.

What must be clarified at the outset are such things as who is responsible for your goods at each stage of their journey and the limit of their liability. Every eventuality should be covered, especially between 'points', such as loading and unloading at docksides. If your crate is dropped, who pays the bill?

If a C.i.f. price has been agreed upon, make sure that the policy (or a certificate) travels with the items and that the description corresponds precisely with the invoice.

An E.C.G.D. policy will insure you against all risks, including insolvency of the buyer, foreign Government action preventing your money reaching you or any other failure to pay, as well as problems arising due to wars and the like. Over a third of all U.K. exports are insured by E.C.G.D.

It is the policy of the Department to 'put British exporters on level terms with foreign competitors . . . ', and an excellent service is given. It is entirely confidential and the buyer remains unaware of the extent of your cover.

Not quite total cover is offered, since it is felt that the exporter should stand some degree of risk, although this is only between 5% and 10%. You may elect to insure all or only part of your exports, although the premium is a little more expensive if you are selective.

Markets are categorised according to risk, and premiums, therefore, vary from country to country.

The Department maintains regional offices throughout the U.K. and is fed information by representatives abroad as well as by our Embassies and Consulates.

Freeports

A freeport is an enclosed zone within or adjacent to a seaport or airport within which goods are treated for customs purposes as being outside the customs territory of the country.

Traders who are registered for V.A.T. purposes are allowed to import goods into a freeport without accounting for tax on them. If they are removed for use in the U.K., then tax becomes due.

The first six experimental freeports are at:

Belfast Airport
Birmingham Airport
Cardiff (close to the docks)
Liverpool docks
Prestwick Airport
Southampton docks

Activities which may take place in a freeport include:

Loading, unloading and trans-shipment
Storage
Sampling, packaging and labelling
Processing of most third country goods for export outside the
    E.E.C.

Benefits include simplified customs procedures, a better cash-flow, economy of scale and a secure environment from the ring fence enclosing the freeport.

CHAPTER 8

Planning and Financial Control

Adopting a Strategy

Every business, large or small, must have a plan. It is as essential to success as is proper utilisation of its resources.

A strategy should therefore be developed. This isn't something that can be decided upon overnight, nor indeed without taking full account of all the many factors which will help to determine it.

You may wonder why a strategy is needed at all. The proof lies in the success of almost every major concern, here and abroad, since corporate planning is now a feature of every type of business, from cakes to computers.

Without it, little companies would not grow big. Earnings would suffer. In a recent United States survey of companies which had developed forward planning, there was a 30% to 40% improvement in their profits.

A strategy needs thinking time and is not something that can be created during a busy working day. It needs sitting on — and sleeping on.

In its absence, the effects of Simon's Law (after Professor H. Simon) are evident: 'Routine drives out planning; the urgent takes priority over the important'.

A well-drawn up plan will assist in meeting crises and sometimes even forestall them. A study of the environment, for instance, in preparation for your plan may highlight potential problem areas long before you would otherwise have met them.

Your decisions will be influenced by many external factors. Legislation is not the least of these, as are fiscal and monetary policies as well as population trends, general price levels, unemployment, technological advances and so on.

A wary eye must be kept on all such influences prior to setting your

MANUAL SYSTEM OR COMPUTER?

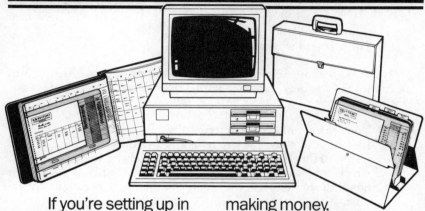

If you're setting up in business, it will pay you to get your book-keeping routines right – right from the start. And you can't do better than Kalamazoo.

Kalamazoo systems have been helping small businesses like yours to prosper and grow for over 80 years. Helping them to save time, reduce costs, and improve cash flow. And leaving them free to concentrate on the really important business of making money.

From the Kalamazoo Small Business Pack (for the smallest business) right through to Kalamazoo business computer systems, we can offer you the system that's right for your business. And one that will grow. As you do.

Kalamazoo
business systems

Northfield, Birmingham B31 2RW
021-475 2191

THE CHOICE IS KALAMAZOO

objectives. Additionally, woven into your final scheme should be the following considerations:

(1) Its consistency, both within your own framework and that of the surrounding environment. Whilst diversification may at times be appropriate, many concerns have come unstuck when moving into an entirely uncomplementary activity. Merely because you make wrought-iron wall brackets does not necessarily entitle you to succeed in making the wooden shelves which rest upon them. This is an entirely different industry.
(2) The degree of risk which you are prepared to take. Your strategy should not include, for example, an all-out market launch of a new product if you are unwilling to commit the necessary resources to its success.
(3) The practical workability of the plan.

How to go about setting your overall objectives then? Taking into account the foregoing, sit down with a large sheet of paper and set out the following:

(1) Your current resources in terms of skills, plant, finance, etc.
(2) List, in your view, the strengths and weaknesses of your current set-up. Honesty is essential here and where weaknesses exist which you would prefer to overlook, nevertheless they must now feature. Ignored, they will raise their ugly heads at a critical time.
(3) The results of your earlier analysis of trends in the areas of commerce and technology and in the social and political fields.
(4) Assess and consider the alternative paths open to the company. Decide which one you want to follow.
(5) Draw up the plans necessary to get you along this road. Break these down into positive programmes and budgets for each of the resources you intend to use.

Once completed, the plan must not be filed away in a dusty drawer. Constantly remind yourself of your goals and evaluate your performance from month to month.

An example of a company pursuing a set strategy is the former Batchelors Peas Ltd. which, recognising that post-war demands pointed to growth in the food industry, moved from canning to a multi-product, multi-technology industry, changing its name to Batchelors Foods Ltd. as part of that plan.

Management Accounts and Budgeting

We have already stressed in Chapter 3 how important it is for every business to operate to a budget. This forms the financial base of the overall strategy and enables management to ensure that things are running to plan.

Budgets have other advantages. They assist in communicating to the various departments the levels of business — and the costs incurred — aimed at by those in overall charge. They help to motivate, for set targets can be seen. And they encourage delegation of responsibility if properly used.

A budget has been defined by W.W. Bigg as 'A financial and/or quantitative statement prepared to a defined period of time of the policy to be pursued during that period for the purpose of attaining a given objective'. A more concise definition would be hard to find.

Budgets must not, however, be rigid. They must cater for some flexibility, either in controllable costs or those outside control. They must also allow for sales or production fluctuations and could, in the latter case for instance, be drawn up for varying levels of productivity between, say, 60% and 100% plus.

Four major areas of budgeting are in common use today:

Sales: This will determine in advance the products to be sold, in which areas and at what price levels. The anticipated related costs will be set down, including direct selling costs as well as those for marketing and distribution.

Production: Manufacture will be regulated to meet the expected demand, as well as controlling material purchases (allowing for wastage), regulating correct quality and quantity levels of labour, and related overheads. This latter item may be broken down again where certain overheads can be identified as forming a disproportionate part of the total.

Expenditure: Budgeting here will ensure that all non-direct costs are known in advance, with each department being made aware of its constraints. Expenses covered will include administration and establishment costs as well as any relating to research and development where these cannot be specifically identified with a particular product.

Financial: This will determine any necessary capital expenditure, control the flow of cash and ensure a satisfactory return on the assets employed within the business.

Examples

Sales Budget (for quarter ending Dec. 19...)

Area	Product X			Product Y			Total £
	Qty.	Price £	Total £	Qty.	Price £	Total £	
Worcestershire	1,000	5	5,000	400	10	4,000	9,000
London	1,200	5	6,000	600	10	6,000	12,000
North East	400	5	2,000	100	10	1,000	3,000
TOTALS	2,600		13,000	1,100		11,000	24,000

Financial Budget (for quarter ending Dec...)

	£	£
New plant required	6,000	
Fixtures and fittings	800	
New vehicle	3,000	9,800
Additional stocks		1,200
Increased debtors during period	1,800	
Less increased creditors	1,000	800
		£11,800

This latter budget reveals that additional funding of £11,800 is needed during this period to meet the anticipated rise in demand.

From the various budgets can be drawn up the Master Budget, incorporating expected sales, production levels, direct and indirect costs, and the level of finance necessary to carry out the operation.

Additionally, it is possible to forecast a Profit and Loss statement for the period covered, as well as a projected Balance Sheet.

All these management tools monitor the success (or otherwise!) of the grand scheme. Differences — known as 'variances' — whether they be favourable or not, must come under investigation. Be satisfied — not complacent — with the causes, or take remedial action.

Of equal importance to management are the trends in the various ratios already covered in Chapter 3. Rising material costs in relation to sales, for instance, require careful investigation of buying policies and the amounts of any scrap going to waste.

One ratio not mentioned earlier is the relationship between the capital employed in the business and the annual sales. The former is basically the net asset position (assets less liabilities) and reveals how effectively they are being used. A falling ratio may indicate under utilisation of certain resources.

Putting Costings to Use

Accepted bases for costing what you have on offer have been explained in Chapter 3. Let us look at the main objects of a proper costing system and the benefits that will accrue to your business by adopting them.

Identifying cost sources enables management to:

(1) Pinpoint cost centres (explained later);
(2) Monitor such costs, using them to expand into the overall budget;
(3) Control them and, in so doing, reduce or eliminate those less effective; and
(4) Assign responsibility in certain areas.

The advantages to management are legion and include:

(1) The identification of the most profitable products or services;
(2) Highlighting areas of waste or loss;
(3) Providing a basis for economies;
(4) Providing useful information in fixing prices (although market forces will, in the long run, decide these); and
(5) Enabling the 'expenses' side of the budget to be drawn up in a systematic manner.

Cost centres are areas where there is a cash outflow and can comprise departments (such as a warehouse or the research and development laboratory), plant and equipment (a machine or a lorry), or a specific person (the Sales Manager and all his related costs).

We have already emphasised the importance of segregating direct (or prime) costs, i.e. those which can be specifically identified with a unit of production, and indirect costs or overheads. This will then enable you to cost on a marginal basis, as outlined in Chapter 3 where each additional widget cost 45p to manufacture. If widgets were sold at £1.45, the remaining £1.00 would go towards fixed costs as well as profit. This is known as the 'contribution'.

As well as the benefits of costing principles above, marginal costing additionally helps management to compare differing levels of production.

A company making sprockets, for instance, may have arrived at a standard cost for each as follows:

Fixed costs   £10,000
Variable (marginal) costs £5 per unit
Anticipated sales   1,000
Total cost = $\frac{£10,000}{1,000}$ = £10 + £5 = £15 per unit

In a competitive market and in the absence of marginal costing knowledge, it may tender for a further order of, say, 100 units at £15 each (plus its normal profit margin), believing it requires this sum to cover costs. But a quote of £13, for instance, still reveals a surplus, *assuming that fixed costs remain static:*

Total sales	£	£
1,000 at £15		15,000
100 at £13		1,300
		16,300
Fixed costs	10,000	
Variable costs	5,500	
(1,100 x £5)		
		15,500
Surplus:		800

Costing of contracts calls for a little more care, particularly when valuing a contract not yet completed.

A popular method is to take as profit into your accounts only work which has been certified and for which payment has been received. This should then be reduced by about one-third to cater for contingencies.

Costing Capital Projects

As a manager of money, one of your most momentous decisions may be whether to give the go-ahead — or the thumbs down — to an expensive new project, probably involving the purchase of several thousand pounds worth of capital assets.

The decision is not always entirely a financial one. Replacement of worn plant may be necessary to meet the requirements of an Act of Parliament or to ease the strain on working conditions.

These benefits cannot easily be quantified but what can be

reasonably measured — in money terms — are the advantages to be gained where increased efficiency and/or greater volume is anticipated.

It is not enough to merely reassure yourself that additional profits, or cost savings, of say, £1,500 per annum can be achieved. Other vital factors may be:

(1) How far ahead have you assessed the benefits? Is there a reasonably certain market in existence for any additional turnover planned?

(2) Will more working capital have to be found? If so, where is the finance coming from?

(3) Has the true cost of borrowing been analysed and is repayment feasible within the expected term?

(4) What additional contribution towards overheads will the new plant provide? (See 'Putting Costings to Use.)

(5) Are the necessary skilled operators available?

Three major formulae exist for quantifying the financial benefits, two of them relatively simple whilst the other, although more sophisticated, takes more factors into account.

Accounting Rate of Return Method (A.R.R.)

This simply measures the yield to the business (after tax and depreciation) against the cost of the original capital employed. The result, averaged over a period, is the rough and ready — and, of course, only anticipated — return.

Let us assume a new grinding machine is to be bought for £5,000 which during its expected five year life will produce additional profits as follows:

Year		
1	£250	
2	500	
3	500	
4	600	
5	650	

Total $\dfrac{£2,500}{5\,\text{yrs}}$ = £500 p.a. average

(Remember that these *additional* profit figures are after allowing for annual depreciation of the machine, thus repaying the original cost)

The A.R.R. is therefore expected to be 10% p.a. (£5,000 divided by £500). Although simple to follow and giving an indication of overall profitability, the method ignores the important 'time value' of money whereby it may be better to receive £500 in Year 2 than £600 in Year 4 since the earlier figure could be reinvested in the business during the following two years to earn further monies.

Payback Method

This simply looks at the time lag before your investment is returned to you in the form of additional savings or earnings. A new press may cost £5,000 and improve profits as follows:

Year	1	£250
	2	500
	3	500
	4	750
	5	1,000
	6	1,500
	7	1,500

It will be seen that at the end of Year 6, £4,500 has been returned to the business and one-third of the way through the following year this will have been topped up to £5,000, the original outlay.

Again easy to follow and one which takes some notice of time, but actual profitability and the cost of capital have been ignored. Also, the formula does not look beyond the payback period to gauge any additional benefits.

Discounted Cash Flow (D.C.F.)

This is the most sophisticated method available at present and one increasingly used throughout commerce and industry.

As well as acknowledging the time value of money, the method reduces — or discounts — future cash receipts to give a 'present value'. This is achieved by the use of easy-to-use tables, giving factors to enable this reduction to be made. Such a table will be found at the end of the book.

If future receipts can be so discounted, they can then be compared with the initial purchase and setting-up costs of any plant involved and a 'net present value' (N.P.V.) emerges. If this is positive, then at the rate of discount used the project should show a profit; a negative net present value indicates a probable loss.

The discount rate chosen obviously determines the outcome of the calculation. What rate should be used?

More often than not, management will lay down a pre-determined rate, being equivalent to, say, the current cost of borrowing capital plus a margin of acceptable profit. This margin will, of course, vary in relation to the degree of risk involved.

Alternatively, no set discount rate may be chosen but the calculation may be carried out on a trial and error basis. You might start, with, say, 11% and produce a positive N.P.V. Trying again with 1% higher may turn this into a negative result and the project, therefore, will produce an 'internal rate of return' somewhere between the two rates. At this point the N.P.V. will be nil, and a decision will have to be made as to whether or not to proceed.

Example

Trial and Error Method
1. Using 11%

Year	Anticipated Earnings	Discount Factor (see table)	Discounted Earnings
1	£1,500	times 0.901	£1,351
2	2,000	0.812	1,624
3	3,000	0.731	2,193
4	4,000	0.659	2,636
5	2,000 plus sale proceeds 2,000 of machine	0.593	2,372
			10,176
		Initial costs, say	10,000
		Positive net present value:	176

2. Using 12%

1	as above	0.893	1,339
2		0.797	1,594
3		0.712	2,136
4		0.635	2,540
5		0.567	2,268
			9,877
			10,000
		Negative net present value:	123

The internal rate of return, therefore, would appear to be about 11.6% p.a.

Alternatively, looking at the first table, it could be said that the project should produce a return of 11% p.a. after repaying the initial costs, as well as resulting in additional profits of £176.

The method can, of course, be applied to two projects to measure which is likely to prove the more profitable.

One word of warning. Such forward projections depend very much on 'guesstimates' of potential profits and we all know how indeterminable these can be. Treat the results, therefore, with caution. Use them as a management tool only.

Controlling Your Stocks

Imagine your stocks to be pound notes. How carefully would you now look after them? Adopt this attitude and your stocks will be accorded the proper treatment they deserve.

Ignore stock control and, in the long run, it will be pound notes that you will be losing.

What do we mean by 'control'? Simply, being aware — by whatever method you find most convenient — of the level and condition at any time of anything purchased or manufactured by your business.

This control starts much earlier than many businessmen realise and does not finish until the goods have finally been converted into hard cash.

Your finger must be on the pulse even before any goods arrive. To run short of supplies could prove at best annoying, at worst disastrous, and therefore stock control encompasses re-ordering and the maintenance of adequate quantities.

Some form of monitoring, therefore, is necessary at various stages: order, receipt, storage, release for production, work in progress, finished goods, warehousing, delivery, payment received.

Simple forms of control can be devised according to the needs of the business. Cards will normally suffice but do ensure they are properly maintained and that the information they show is accurate. If you do this, it will be possible to take a stock count regularly without the need for a time-consuming physical check.

Minimum and maximum levels should be set, as well as the quantity to be re-ordered when the lower level is reached. These figures will naturally depend on usage, as well as the time it takes to obtain new supplies, known as the 'lead' time.

If average lead time for a certain item is, say, 4 weeks, then the minimum level must be set to ensure that enough units remain in stock during this time lag. A careful balance is needed between the danger of running short and the known expense of overstocking. Money tied up in stock is not working to the benefit of the business.

Apart from the actual cost of buying required stock, whether raw materials, part-finished or completed goods, other expenses are involved and it has been estimated that stock can cost up to 20% of its basic value merely to hold.

There may be financing charges, costs relating to purchase, losses on damaged or obsolescent items, handling and paperwork expenditure, and storage payments.

For this reason it is essential to turn your stock over as frequently as you can. This releases working capital, the lifeblood of any business.

Slow selling items must not be allowed to interfere with this flow. If your control is efficient, periodic checks will soon reveal those lines not selling quickly enough to justify their retention and evasive action must be taken.

One big United States drapery chain sets maximum time limits for each line. Any left at the end of the period are immediately reduced in price by up to 75% Whilst some losses result, the goods are speedily turned into cash, enabling the stores to move quickly into the next fashion line.

The importance of stock control cannot be over emphasised and it is, of course, a vital cog in the chain of strategy. You will have already set anticipated demand levels and part way along that curve is not the time to meet supply problems. Keep a record of all raw material and parts sources and be one step ahead if an emergency arises.

Stock Valuations

Certain rules exist governing the timing and method of valuing your stocks, including raw materials and work in progress.

Annual valuations will almost certainly be required to comply with accountancy standards but any efficient business would not dream of leaving such a long gap between checks.

Regular physical counts are not essential. It will often be found that a large proportion of the value of stocks is tied up in a minority percentage. Find which are the most valuable and only these may require physically counting, say quarterly.

Pareto's Law, met earlier, exists here also, suggesting that invariably 20% of stocks account for 80% of the total value. It is upon that 20% which you should concentrate your attention, for that is where most of your money is lying.

When taking stock, remember that accountancy standards require you to value at the lower of cost or net realisable value in each case. Cost may include prime costs and any expenditure involved in bringing the goods to their current location and condition, including a fair proportion of overheads. But if the true market value, i.e. net realisable value, has fallen below this cost, then the smaller of the two figures has to be allocated.

Various methods of valuation exist where goods are being bought in and sold again. The two major ones are 'First In, First Out' (FIFO) and 'Average'. The former calculates that the first item in any range sold can be taken as being the first of that type purchased, so that stock is represented by those more latterly bought. Averaging is merely the calculation of middle purchase and sales prices. FIFO is probably the better method for small businesses.

Manufacturing concerns may use differing bases, dependent upon costing procedures. Full costing will throw up very different figures from marginal costing, although true profits cannot vary. One period's 'excess' will simply be reflected in the figures for the following period.

What is more important is to get the valuations right in the first place and adhere to the same rules as time goes on. Closing stock values (which are next period's opening figures) affect gross profit and any under- or over-valuing will therefore be carried down to the net profit line, distorting the true figures. This can be seen in this example:

	£		£		£
Sales	50,000		50,000		50,000
Opening Stock	20,000	20,000		20,000	
Purchases	20,000	20,000		20,000	
	40,000	40,000		40,000	
Closing Stock	20,000	15,000		25,000	
Cost of Goods Sold	20,000		25,000		15,000
Gross profit	30,000		25,000		35,000

Assuming £20,000 to be a fair valuation of the closing stock position, then a £5,000 under-valuation reduces — or appears to reduce — gross profit. Similarly, a £5,000 over-valuation distorts the figures and suggests gross profit this much higher. (Direct labour or other direct costs have been ignored for simplification.)

You can see the importance, therefore, of applying true values to stocks, not only to produce figures of worthwhile value to the business, but, just as important, to calculate the correct taxation charge.

Research and Development

This is not, as you might think, something just for the big boys. Time spent on researching and developing your product or service is equally as important to the smaller company, especially in a technical or competitive area. Keep ahead of the market and you will be one step in front of your competitors. Some larger groups spend as much as 15/20% of their turnover on research.

Rapid technological advances make some goods obsolescent only a year or two after production commences and you don't want to be caught napping. Additionally the increasing trend towards diversification brings many new firms into industries where research has suggested to them that profits are to be made.

Obviously your own capabilities for research may be limited. Examine firstly:

(1) Your existing resources, in the shape of quality and numbers of suitable staff;
(2) What costs you are prepared to lay out;
(3) The specialist fields which you are able to cover; and
(4) Your own product life-cycles, for timing of introduction will in turn affect earlier research programmes.

If research is out of the question, at this stage at least, then all is not lost. Several specialised Research Units exist where advice and co-operation can be found. These include the National Engineering Laboratory and the National Physical Laboratory.

Also ready to serve you — although at a cost in most cases — are such member bodies as the Electrical Research Association, the Furniture Industry Research Association, the Production Engineering Research Association and the Machine Tool Industry Research Association.

There are, indeed, many more, each allied to a particular industry and a complete list is available at most reference libraries under the title 'Technical Services for Industry'.

Such associations often run open days and offer many technical and library services to members. Certain facilities are usually available to non-members for a fee.

CHAPTER 9

Obtaining Further Finance

Introduction

We have already reviewed in Chapter 3 the major sources of finance available to new concerns and, of course, these same sources continue to supply funds as a business grows.

Once established, however, additional methods of raising money may become available to you, such as factoring, discussed in Chapter 11. Leasing is also more easily arranged once you have a sound balance sheet to show to a prospective lessor.

But before looking outside the business, satisfy yourself that every effort is being made to generate cash internally, for this is by far the cheapest way of improving your working capital. For instance:

Are profits being retained in the company or are they being drawn out at perhaps an over-excessive rate?

Can debtors be pressed for more prompt payment? Check on the average days outstanding (see Chapter 3, ratio 5a) and see by how much this can be improved. As an example, if annual sales are £100,000 and average debtors £20,000, this gives an average days' outstanding period of 73. A 10-day improvement means a one-off cash injection into the business of some £2,700, i.e.

$$£20,000 \text{ minus } \frac{£100,000 \times 63 \text{ days}}{365}$$

Could you alter your terms of business — and still remain competitive?

Are you taking full advantage of credit terms from your suppliers and other creditors? Whilst you must not prejudice good relations, it may well be possible to arrange slightly longer credit.

Can you reduce stocks of raw materials, work-in-progress or finished goods? (See Chapter 8, 'Controlling Your Stocks'.)

Would a different method of distribution help?

Could capital expenditure be reduced or delayed?

Can a cash advance be arranged with major customers to finance a particular order?

Are shareholders or partners prepared to invest a little more in the business?

If you are losing money, is it being so 'arranged' in the most tax effective manner? Here, your accountant obviously needs to be called in.

Re-examine your cost structure.

Calculate the potential for price increases.

Take a detailed look at any discounts you offer. A 5% offer for payments within 30 instead of, say, 60 days means *you* are giving money away at over 60% on an annual basis!

Having exhaused these possibilities, reached your limits on overdraft or loan, and taken a look at hire purchase, leasing and factoring, on what else can you fall back in the event of requiring further finance? Exports are especially catered for by E.C.G.D. (See Chapter 7). Further shares may be issued if you run a limited company although the subscribers may expect a say in the running of things. Alternatively, it may be possible to issue a Debenture, a special type of loan to a limited concern, but you will probably need some solid assets to back this up. What else is available?

Mortgaging Property

Long-term funds can sometimes be obtained from an insurance company or a building society for industrial use where a freehold or long (say over 20 years) leasehold can be offered as collateral.

Only a proportion of current market value will become available, perhaps 70%. If a 'sale and leaseback' can be arranged, however, a sum in excess of the market price may be arranged, based on the value of the annual rent to be paid.

As well as insurance companies, some financial trusts, property investment companies and pension funds offer a similar service.

Specialist Concerns

Merchant banks are prepared to finance carefully selected private companies where funds of in excess of £25,000 are needed. They will almost certainly seek part of the equity (but only a minority) and may require that regular dividends be paid after an initial period.

Their interest is usually long term and they will help in the management of a concern until, eventually, a public flotation of its shares becomes a possibility.

The larger merchant banks are members of the Accepting Houses Committee and in this connection they also finance the more progressive and profitable companies by giving support to bills issued by them.

There are also several venture capital specialists such as the Small Business Capital Fund and Charterhouse Development who, in return for a non-executive seat on the board, and perhaps a minority shareholding, will arrange loans, usually in excess of £50,000 although a good profit record is essential.

A growing number of financial institutions are members of the British Venture Capital Association, set up in an effort to formalise standards in this fast growing area.

The former National Enterprise Board and the National Research Development Corporation now come under the umbrella of the British Technology Group which concentrates on supporting technological innovation. Its two main schemes incorporate Oakwood Loan Finance and the Small Company Innovation Fund.

Oakwood offers unsecured five-year loans of up to £50,000 for businesses in England and repayment is not called for until the fourth year of the loan. B.T.G. usually takes an option to purchase up to 20% of the equity at current market prices, although the owners also have the right to buy out this option.

The Small Company Innovation Fund provides finance for innovative companies throughout the U.K. to a maximum of £60,000.

B.T.G. has also linked itself to English Industrial Estates to offer a joint package involving finance and factory space known as Acorn.

A further scheme allows B.T.G. to invest up to £100,000 in a company whereby repayment is effected through a levy on sales.

Inventors should consider approaching B.T.G. which has a record of helping all types of concerns, including everything from furniture to seaside rock. The Group also operates as an information exchange and 'marriage bureau' between inventors and companies seeking innovations.

I.C.F.C. and T.D.C. have already been looked at in Chapter 3 but are worthy of further consideration by you now if your circumstances have, as we hope, changed. I.C.F.C. is today the major source of term finance for Britain's smaller companies. A 10-year survey showed that concerns assisted by the Corporation achieved a growth rate of 150% compared with only 83% amongst companies as a whole, highlighting the management expertise that is 'bought' when loans are arranged.

Run by I.C.F.C. is the Estate Duties Investment Trust (EDITH) whose object is to assist companies in financial difficulty because of the death of a major shareholder, although it will also buy out personal holdings. The Trust purchases the shares (£5,000 to £1m.), which might otherwise be difficult to dispose of, and enables the company to continue an uninterrupted existence.

Investment Trusts are taking a closer look at progressive family businesses and funds can now be made available from this source.

For the agriculturist there is the Agricultural Mortgage Corporation, one of the most prolific suppliers of long-term finance for farmers, often for periods of 40 years or more. Then there are the Agricultural Credit Corporation, who are sometimes prepared to guarantee bank borrowings, and the Lands Improvement Company, where up to 40 year money is made available for capital improvements to farms. The Land Settlement Association Ltd. can assist with initial working capital.

Local schemes exist up and down the country, such as the St. Helen's Trust on Merseyside, set up by Pilkingtons to provide over £1m for investment in small concerns.

The four major Clearing Banks are all contributing towards help for small businesses. Barclays and Midland are involved with the London Enterprise Agency; the Midland has launched a venture capital fund and participates in Moracrest and Meritor Investments; the National Westminster, through its Growth Options offshoot, is experimenting with unsecured start-up loans in the Black Country; and Lloyds has launched its special Business Loans, specifically aimed at smaller and medium-sized concerns. Its Pegasus subsidiary provides venture capital.

Even the Post Office (through its Superannuation Scheme) is now prepared to inject funds (up to £100,000 in each case) in small companies. Initial 'vetting' is carried out by the Small Firms Information Service.

The National Coal Board is also investing in small business and again up to £100,000 in each instance is available through its pension management division.

Government Assistance

Some of the financial benefits that can be obtained through Government or quasi-Government means have already been explained in Chapter 3. Schemes tend to come and go and it is essential that you check up on the latest availability *before* committing yourself. If you deal with one of the major accountancy firms, they will usually have a specialist on their staff to help you; alternatively your Federation or Chamber of Commerce may assist.

A major review of assisted areas recently took place, cutting the number from three to two as follows:

Development areas which are eligible for regional development grants at 15% and also for selective assistance; and

Intermediate areas, eligible for selective assistance only.

Regional development grants are given towards the cost of new buildings, plant and equipment. Selective assistance is negotiable and the Government will pay only the minimum necessary for the project to go ahead.

There are normally four basic conditions:

(1) The project must be of some national (as opposed to local, and hence such businesses as 'corner shops' are excluded) benefit.
(2) The project must create or preserve jobs.
(3) You must stand a reasonable chance of completing the project successfully, i.e. you hold the necessary management and technical skills, manpower and finance.
(4) The grant must make something happen. So do not start until you have the go-ahead!

Capital grants are subject to a cost-per-job limit of £10,000, although if the project is labour-intensive there can be a grant of £3,000 for each new job created. Further, small firms are not subject to these limits.

There are also a number of government aid schemes aimed at specific industry sectors, although these are subject to change at very short notice and, again, you are advised to check. They include:

CADCAM (Computer-aided design/manufacturing), which offers grants of up to one-third of eligible project costs, including consultants' reports.

Support for Innovation Scheme, designed to improve the technological base of U.K. industry and to help companies put improved products and processes onto the market more quickly and effectively. All sectors of manufacturing industry can claim benefit.

Robot Advisory Service to support the advance of robotics in industry.

Software Products Scheme which offers grants or shared cost contracts to computer service companies.

Microelectronics Industry Support Programme, for grants aimed primarily at the development, production and use of microelectronic components.

Design Advisory Service provides free consultancy advice on all aspects of design, however small the company involved.

Quality Assurance Advisory Scheme, to assist on setting proper standards of production.

Information Technology Centres, of which there are nearly 200 in the U.K.

As well as these home-produced incentives, as members of the Common Market, businessmen in the U.K. are entitled to consideration within much wider geographical schemes.

Of most interest to smaller firms are the European Investment Bank which arranges loans of £17,000 upwards over 7 years and the Community's Agricultural Fund for large projects of an agricultural nature. Loans of up to £1m are now available on special terms to smaller companies in run-down coal and steel areas as a result of an aid scheme between the Department of Industry and the European Coal and Steel Community. The Community will lend up to 50% of the fixed asset cost of projects which create new jobs for former coal and steel workers.

Help can also be sought from your local authority (particularly New Towns) who have limited scope to grant aid when new jobs are being created within their boundaries.

The British Steel Corporation has set up a subsidiary in order to ease the running down of some of its mills. It passes on benefits such as empty buildings and surplus labour to businesses able to make use of such resources.

Massive Governmental assistance is also available for companies and environmental projects in steel, shipbuilding and textile areas, and this is especially aimed at smaller concerns.

Most of the cash comes from the European Community's regional development fund and assistance is in addition to our own Government spending.

Money from this fund can be obtained for a variety of purposes, including, for instance, the conversion of old buildings into suitable premises for small businesses. The intention is to help restructure regions hit by community policies affecting the declining steel, shipbuilding and textile industries. Most of the grants to smaller concerns are likely to go towards buying professional consultancy advice, and will be given in relatively small amounts.

The areas particularly benefiting are:

Strathclyde	South & West Yorkshire
Cleveland	Workington
Clwyd	Tyne & Wear
S. Glamorgan	Merseyside
Gwent	Belfast
Corby	Tayside
Durham	Lancashire
Humberside	Greater Manchester

Presenting Your Case

In any of these schemes, the ultimate decision rests with an individual or a committee. In either case he, she or they are going to be influenced in part by the way in which you put forward your request for assistance.

Disjointed notes and figures on scraps of paper are not very likely to help your case. This is a supreme example of having to 'sell' yourself, whether it be personally or through a written application for funds.

If you are at all unsure about your ability to present the information in a cogent and clear manner, do not hesitate to seek professional advice. This may be from your accountant, solicitor, banker or a firm specialising in such matters, as many industrial consultants for instance do. Ask the Institute of Management Consultants for their register of members.

It may cost you a few hundred pounds but, being an entrepreneur, you are already aware of the need to speculate to accumulate and if such a small investment can recoup several thousands of pounds by way of grant or subsidised loan, the outlay will have been more than worthwhile.

Very often it will only be necessary to complete a form, or set of forms, although additional information may be called for and it is here that correct layout and sophisticated presentation will help to ensure success.

No standard procedure can be recommended but consider all of the following aspects, discard those that appear irrelevant and reconstruct the remainder in the most logical manner apparent to your needs:

(a) Brief summary of the business.
(b) Recent set of *audited* accounts.
(c) Summary of past trading results, with reasons for any unusual trends.
(d) Details and experience of senior management.
(e) Company objectives, both short and long term.
(f) Projections (sales, gross profit, overheads, net profit) for the next 2/3 years.
(g) Current and potential markets.
(h) Details of major competition — known and expected.
(i) Current order schedule.
(j) Financing requirements with a Cash Budget and repayment programme.
(k) Product details and anticipated developments.
(l) Cost and price structures along with market influences on the latter.
(m)Export potential.

(n) Distribution channels.
(o) Prime cost resources in terms of labour and materials anticipated requirements.
(p) Legislation affecting or likely to affect sales.

The whole package should be typed, indexed and preferably bound, with several copies made available. Photographs of location and your products can only help to achieve success.

Danger Signs

In all your financing considerations, never lose sight of the twin spectres of under-capitalisation and overtrading.

These horrors often go together because, although they do not mean quite the same thing, they stem from a common source, i.e. shortage of proprietors' funds in the business.

A trading entity is rather like an upturned pyramid, with sales represented by the upper horizontal line and capital by the bottom 'point'. If the point is too weak to support the remainder, it will topple over — into the bankruptcy or liquidation courts.

A fine balance needs to be maintained for it is nearly as important (although less dangerous) to make sure there is not an abundance of under-utilised capital in the form of wasting or costly assets.

Under-capitalisation can lead to inadequate supplies of raw materials and subsequent disruptions to production and delivery; lost opportunities; and forcibly expensive buying procedures. An over-ambitious business may follow a policy of going for increasing volume sales and overtrading is likely to ensue. Outside borrowings increase until the stage is reached where interest and capital repayment demands force a showdown.

Never allow your business to reach even the margins of these deadly shores.

One way of checking on safety is the method known as capital gearing, i.e. the relationship between shareholders' funds (on which no interest is 'demanded') and fixed-interest borrowings.

If the greater proportion of the company's capital is represented by fixed-interest loans it is said to have a high gearing; conversely a low gearing is in force where shareholders' monies represent the majority of the capital.

There are, naturally, serious risks in building up a large fixed-interest portfolio, especially if profitability is subject to volatile fluctuations and it goes through a bad patch. The lenders will still demand their interest!

Where fixed-interest loans are in being, profit levels (before interest and taxation) must adequately cover the annual interest charge and some accountants would suggest these need to be at least three times the outgoing figure, although this may have to be even more fully covered under certain circumstances.

Fixed-interest items in this context may relate to debentures or certain preference shares as well as to commercial loans.

'Gearing' is a loosely-used term and is sometimes applied to the relationship between debt (loans, debentures, hire purchase, bank borrowings, etc.) and equity (shareholders' funds).

No ideal rules can be laid down but, as a guide only, equity should normally be no more than debt and, preferably, somewhat in excess of it.

Always seek professional financial advice before restructuring capital or arranging increased borrowings and don't let your company fall into the under-capitalisation trap.

Further Reading

Leading firms of chartered accountants produce excellent brochures on many aspects of business, obtainable from any of their offices. Arthur Young (Rolls House, 7 Rolls Building, Fetter Lane, London EC4A 1NL) provide a summary to public assistance entitled *Financial Incentives and Assistance for Industry*, whilst Peat, Marwick Mitchell & Co. (1 Puddle Duck, Blackfriars, London EC4V 3PD) make available a host of publications including *Business Start-up Scheme*, *Debt Factoring* and a fact-packed guide to Government incentives entitled *Finance for New Projects in the U.K.* Telford Development Corporation (with Wrekin Council) (T.D.C., Priorslee Hall, Telford, Shropshire TF2 9NT) have available a wide series of Fact Sheets, useful wherever you may be based. Strathclyde University (Centre for the study of Public Policy) have produced a work which encompasses all of the industrial aids available to business in the U.K.

A very readable guide to grants and loans available within the European Community entitled *Finance from Europe* is published by the London Office of the Commission of the European Communities.

CHAPTER 10

The Importance of People

Introduction

Of all the resources at your fingertips, the most remunerative to your business in terms of increased productivity can be the people you employ. Your attitude towards labour, from prior to recruitment to the time they are drawing a pension, could be the determining factor between success, mediocrity or, at worst, failure.

The personnel management function is probably more important in the smaller firm than in the larger one, where specialists in this sphere are normally employed. In a 'one-man business' you have to be managing director, sales director, finance director and perhaps production director — at least initially.

What you must not overlook, however, is that you will also be personnel director. How should you tackle this aspect of the business?

Having the Right Mix

Assuming that it has been within your control from the word 'go', you can do no better than start with the right people. In numbers, in quality and in mix.

As part of your initial strategy, you should decide by what calibre of people your organisation will best be served. Ignore limitations of supply at this stage: concentrate on requirements.

If you are going to be selling high technology products, this will naturally demand technical brains somewhere in the outfit, Quality and cost of your product or service may call for varying degrees of intelligence or numeracy in your workforce.

Selling by telephone will be more successfully carried out by someone naturally responsive and articulate than by the shy, retiring type. 'Avon' ladies are chosen for particular attributes just as much as computer analysts. And so on ....

The recruitment of a sensibly balanced workforce will be the result

of correctly forecasting both the needs of your company and those of
your hoped-for customers.

Manpower planning is a continuing art. It begins when you decide
to go it alone in business and should be constantly reviewed in the light
of progress and growth.

Never allow duplication of manpower, for this is where costs will
start to bite. Be on the alert, therefore, for signs of overlapping and
check for this from time to time.

Never allow additions to the management structure without prior
scrutiny of the need. It is invariably more difficult — and more painful
— to attempt cutbacks at senior levels than at production and clerical
level.

The appointment of senior personnel, whether by promotion or
recruitment, should always follow a close review of the resultant
delegation and authority patterns rather than being an easy, although
costly, answer to what may be a temporary over-worked problem.
You may end up with too many Chiefs for the appointed number of
Indians!

As an aid to intelligent future manpower requirements, two simple
sets of records should be maintained.

Constant up-dating of these is not necessary but each should be
carefully looked at and amended as necessary prior to periodic staff
reviews.

The first set, maintained in alphabetical order, should record as a
minimum the following details of each employee, from the most
humble to management:

Name and present position
Date of birth and present age(*)
Qualifications
Date of joining and length of service(*)
Time in present position(*)
Years to retirement(*)
Considered potential   (*) record in pencil and amend annually

The second set should define each job within the organisation:

Description
Preferred age range
Educational competence necessary
Professional qualifications necessary
Experience and/or any special skills required
Personal attributes necessary
Possible promotion to?

Reviews of these records, at least annually and independently of staff assessment considerations, will help to identify future needs as well as providing the names of the most likely candidates.

Several alternative solutions to changing requirements within the manpower planning programme may be available to you and only a blend of your own experience and intuition will help you in choosing the correct ones. These may include:

(1) Advertising for further employees
(2) Arranging transfers and promotions within the company
(3) Redundancy programmes
(4) Arranging suitable training or re-training schemes
(5) Early retirements, or continuing to employ people after normal retiring age
(6) Moving the workplace
(7) Restructuring salary schemes; introducing incentives
(8) Improving performance through increased productivity, following the use of work-study or organisation and method techniques
(9) Engaging temporary or part-time staff, or changing the nature of shift work.

Defining Each Job

Ask the average employee to tell you *exactly* what he is expected to achieve, to whom he is responsible and precisely the limits of his own authority and responsibility — and many would face a difficult task in providing a full answer.

Job description and definition, however, is becoming increasingly accepted throughout service and manufacturing industries, as well as commerce, for the important part it plays in determining and maintaining good morale levels amongst employees.

Decide even *before* you advertise for a new employee his precise tasks, authority and responsibility — and you should end up with a contented workforce. Ignoring these guidelines may land you with staff frustrated in their day-to-day work as well as their ultimate ambitions. The adverse effect on your business can be imagined.

Draw up a diagram of each working position in this manner:

TITLE
Immediately responsible to
Main functions: *
Specific tasks:

Delegatory powers to: Responsible for
          *   *

Authority for Within the organisation:
Relations with outsiders:

Resources for which responsible: Fixed assets
Working assets:
Financial:
Manpower:
((*) names of superiors and subordinates)

Discuss each aspect with the appropriate employee and ensure that he is supplied with a copy. There should be no overlapping of responsibility, nor anything other than clear understanding of authority. An employee should *never* report to more than one superior.

These definitions must, of course, remain flexible as the business expands but no alterations should be made without first being fully explained (with reasons) to the employee concerned.

A positive reporting system is essential in any business and the laid down procedure must be clear to all. Properly followed, it should ensure rapid identification of potential problems, which can then be dealt with before any serious disruption of business relations occurs.

Encourage employees to report problems, however minor, to their next-in-line. Don't forget to praise them when they spot something to the firm's advantage, and reward where appropriate.

Knowing precisely what each employee has to do and how he has to do it will enable you to carry out the next important step in creating a workforce superior to that of your competitors.

Setting Objectives

We have already seen how an overall strategy for the business will guide it along its intended path.

As part of that plan, break down your ultimate goals so as to set individual, or departmental, targets in line with them.

Every business will act differently and it is difficult to suggest any set pattern. But, naturally, those responsible for sales can agree (after consultation) targets to meet each period (monthly, four-weekly, quarterly, etc.); the production team can set cycle times or quantity per hour or day figures; administrative workers can be given ideals to complete in any particular period; delivery men similar targets and so on.

The targets must be achievable, as well as being flexible to meet situation changes. They must also be agreed beforehand.

There is little point in haranguing workers for not meeting

objectives if, for instance, spasmodic raw material supplies have upset production. More importantly, however, is the fact that you will have two sets of figures to compare, i.e. target and actual. Variances can be analysed and, when reasons are not fully known, further investigated.

Let each and every worker know the part he is playing in an overall objective or budget. These may relate to achievements, or limiting expenditure, both vital components of your final profit figure.

Telling is not enough. If you know that 840 widgets have to be produced weekly to meet fixed costs alone, explain the reasons fully. Say *why* this number must be turned out and, if necessary, *how*.

Lack of proper communication between management and workers is considered to be the cause behind many major strikes which, on the surface appear to have other reasons behind them. Don't let it happen in *your* business.

Try this 5-point plan:

(1) Advise — what you expect
(2) Plan (together) — how it can be achieved
(3) Inform — people of progress
(4) Guide — where shortfalls exist; and
(5) Reward — when targets are met.

Rewards do not have to be monetary and, of course, legislation may preclude this:

There are two major theories about why people work and, although actually more complex, they reduce to:

(1) Because they must, to provide basic needs; and
(2) Because work itself is a need and can be a satisfying experience.

No doubt the 'true' answer lies somewhere between the two, although there is little doubt that, with the vastly improved working conditions seen during this century, many millions of employees are quite satisfied with their work — as opposed, of course, to their pay!

The right salary levels help to keep people satisfied and these you will have to regularly review. Keep in mind other methods of improving your employees' take-home pay such as incentive and productivity schemes as well as profit-sharing.

Consider competitions, although make sure that rivalry stays on a friendly level. Try to base any contest targets on profits made rather than on turnover, which may not in fact be producing a profit!

Having made it clear to each employee exactly what his place is in the organisation, how do you try to keep him happy?

Looking After Employees

From the moment they arrive on their first morning at work, they should feel part of the place around them. It is your job to see that a carefully planned induction programme begins.

The answers given to such simple problems as where to hang their coats or where to buy lunch can make or mar their first day — and so, perhaps, their lasting impression.

Delegate someone, preferably of their own age range and sex, to help them along for the first week or two. Make sure their supervision is effective and that someone is always available to answer their queries.

Properly inducted, that new member of staff will quickly join the ranks of contented people already working for you.

The progress of all employees should be reviewed fully, at least annually, with preferably mini-reviews at six-monthly intervals.

A standard Report Form should be devised, with either a marking system (say 0 to 5) or comments upon at least these attributes:

Personality	Initiative
Leadership	Team Spirit
Efficiency	Communicative Ability
Accuracy	Appearance
Judgement	Potential

Marks are preferable to comments since they clearly show improvement or a worsening situation. Vague terms like 'adequate' or 'satisfactory' can have a variety of meanings and are not recommended.

Discuss the report, once completed, with the employee in undisturbed surroundings. Welcome his views and take a written note of any particularly appropriate comments so that these can be reviewed at the next assessment.

Working conditions are more important to staff than many employers recognise. It is silly to lose a good typist merely for the sake of providing her with a new chair or a warmer office. Yet many people change their jobs for such apparently minor reasons without ever bringing them to the attention of the business.

Maintain a system of regularly walking around your place of work, say monthly. Look the place over with a refreshed eye, as would a visitor for the first time.

Why is that 'Fire-Door' always propped open? Why hasn't that cracked window been mended yet? Is it time Mr. Bloggs had a larger desk? And what about having that telephone moved so that Miss Foggit can reach it without having to leave her chair every time?

Check the layout. Listen for undue noise. Look at cleanliness.

Try a system of job rotation. This cannot be worked everywhere but, where it is possible, can reduce boredom, increase efficiency and keep people happier.

Don't overlook the social side of your employees' lives. Would they welcome an annual get-together, perhaps with partners? Could lunch time activities, such as darts or table tennis, help to maintain a friendly atmosphere?

Holiday priorities are considered important and this may well provide you with some problems. Employees with children at school will probably expect their holidays to coincide and some careful juggling may be necessary. Although your prime duty is to your customers, your business won't get very far with dissatisfied staff!

The possibility of appointing worker-directors should be given some thought, although clear lines of authority will have to be worked out if a scheme is proposed.

Most families try to save money regularly and a savings scheme may be welcomed. Deductions can easily — and, for the employee, painlessly — be made direct from wage or salary and placed in an interest-bearing deposit. Such funds are trust monies and must be closely guarded.

Never overlook staff suggestions and, if there is a demand, set up a formal procedure with rewards in appropriate cases. Many larger firms save thousands of pounds annually by running such schemes.

Particularly identify your key employees, those where their long-term absence could disrupt business. If you are quite satisfied with their progress, make them completely aware of this. Reward as necessary.

All appropriate staff should be aware of possible promotion patterns. Be ready to willingly discuss horizons with anyone who approaches you on this subject.

An employee's aims, ideals and needs, once known, can often be met in the longer term. Unknown, they simply remain bottled up causing unhappiness and frustration.

As a good employer, you will also be concerned with their health and welfare. Help where you can and benefit will be twofold.

Canteen facilities, especially on a subsidised basis, can prove as beneficial to the business as to those who use them; a well-fed, rested employee works better in the afternoons!

Fringe benefits could include:

pensions, life assurance, day release, tuition fees, medical insurance, flexible working hours, social facilities, season ticket loans, clothing and hairdressing allowances, assistance with house purchase, canteens, maternity benefits, cars, discount purchasing, share incentives, etc.

Sometimes interviews will be less pleasant and matters of discipline will come your way for discussion and decision. Play fair and you will be doing your best.

Constant lateness, poor work, and so on should be dealt with firmly and at an early stage. Bad habits, if not checked, can become contagious. Before you know it, you could have a sloppy workforce on your hands.

More serious matters of discipline are dealt with in Chapter 5.

Staff Training

Why train staff? Training is time-consuming and therefore costly. Surely a new recruit can simply learn as he goes along, picking up new techniques on the way?

This is certainly one way of 'teaching' new workers the ways and whims of your firm. But it is not the best way.

This rather casual method ensures only that they learn to do things the way their 'tutor' does them, which may leave room for improvement. They learn by practice, and whilst this has to be included in any type of programme, what they may miss is *why* they are doing what they are.

Too much theory leads only to boredom but enough to explain the practice will prove of long-lasting benefit both to the employee and the firm.

A proper training programme should be drawn up for every employee, including management.

Let the trainee know what you have planned for him in the coming year. An ideal time to do this is following discussion of his annual assessment.

Make full use of the Training Board allied to your industry. Find out about specialist courses run by the many centres up and down the country.

They may cost you money but there is little doubt that such expense is more than offset by the resultant staff satisfaction levels and, of course, improved customer relations.

The benefits of training are now widely recognised throughout industry. In the retailing field we are all familiar with such leaders as Marks and Spencer's signs proclaiming later opening times once a week, when this period is used for training purposes.

Each company's needs will differ. To gauge yours, ask yourself:

(1) What type of training needs to be done? Is it administrative, financial, technical, managerial, etc?
(2) What tutorial resources do we have?
(3) What outside resources need to be used?
(4) How much time and money need to be allocated to the task?
(5) How do we intend to evaluate the results?

This final point must not be overlooked, for as well as acting as a measure of success, an evaluation will help to keep your methods of training in line with your objectives.

Design your training to cover:

(1) Coping with the technical demands of the job,
(2) Providing background information;
(3) Teaching the necessary techniques and their best form of application;
(4) Leadership requirements; and
(5) Adapting to changing conditions.

Don't expect to see instant results following a sustained period of training. Like good wine, employees take time to mature. Longer-term benefits are of more importance than immediate post-training results.

Always decide upon the expected level of attainment, which should conform to the needs of the company rather than anticipated staff capabilities.

Most employees will stretch their normal boundaries if they feel they are playing a planned part in an overall campaign of self-advancement.

Training *methods* are important and, for this reason, specialists are advised for the smaller firm, where neither the time nor the expertise usually exist.

Trainees must be given an opportunity to practise at an early stage, and not simply be allowed to watch, listen or read, depending upon the initial theoretical approach in use.

Whilst a background of mechanical drawing knowledge is essential for the draughtsman under training, don't be afraid of letting him loose in the first week or two with a sheet of drawing paper and a pencil. Similarly, anyone learning to use a machine should be given an opportunity, with the proper safeguards, of at least appreciating the difficulties early in his training!

Properly planned and evaluated, training should ensure several advantages, not the least of them being:

(1) An eventual saving in time and money;
(2) A greater respect for the 'tools of the trade' under the charge of the trainee;
(3) An improvement in morale;
(4) A better customer relationship; and
(5) A reduced staff turnover rate, culminating in further savings.

Job Efficiency

Two differing attitudes exist to the way in which any operation — mechanical, administrative, etc, — is carried out.

One is the 'Adam and Eve' syndrome, i.e. 'It has always been done that way'. The other more enlightened and progressive asks: 'Is there a better way of doing it? Or even: 'Does it need to be done at all?'

Surveys of clerical procedures in industrial environments invariably reveal a horrifying proportion of duplication. Worse still, the preparation of many statistics for which no-one can justify any real use often comes to light!

A motto above your desk that 'Jobs take time — and time means money' may act as a continuing reminder of the necessity of reassessing every operation in your concern on a regular basis.

This discipline, fully accepted by big concerns, is just as important for the smaller firm. It comes under many guises, including Work Study, Work Measurement, and Organisation and Method Study.

Whatever you call it, don't ignore it. The complexity of modern industry and commerce demands its use and, providing its introduction is dealt with sensibly, it should be accepted by your workforce.

Keep everyone in the picture, discuss the implications and show how increased productivity is beneficial to all — even easier if you have a profit-sharing scheme!

Gaining popularity are the formation of 'Quality Circles', small groups of people who do similar work in an organisation, meeting regularly in company time to identify, analyse and solve localised problems.

Common fears, such as loss of jobs or lower pay, are normally groundless but, nevertheless, must be dealt with sympathetically and truthfully. Advantages are limitless, but include:

(1) A reduction in costs,
(2) The conversion of this benefit to increased profits, lower selling prices and/or higher wages;
(3) More efficient control by management;
(4) Improved service to customers;
(5) Greater job satisfaction;
(6) Easier supervision; and
(7) The elimination of unnecessary work.

Work Study is a specialist's job and someone with proper grounding should preferably be used. Failing this in the smaller firm, a basic study of the methods used and their application should enable some experimentation to take place. Common sense is at the root in, for instance, detailing the right procedure:

(1) Define the problem to be undertaken;
(2) Record the facts as they currently exist;
(3) Examine these with a view to seeking improvements;
(4) Put these into practice;
(5) Monitor performance and make factual comparison with 2 above;
(6) Further improve where possible and draw up new guidelines;
(7) Monitor these, with regular reviews.

At all times keep your employees informed. Seek alternative suggestions from them.

Question *everything* about each operation. What is its purpose? How is this achieved? Where? When? By Whom? At what cost? At what risk?

Look at every feature — layout, material handling, conditions, plant usage, tools required, storage, etc.

These practices apply as much to office procedures, where they are usually known as Organisation and Method Study, as to production processes.

Benefits may thus be seen in all departments, leading to growth and eventually the possibility of expansion.

CHAPTER 11

Growing Larger

Introduction

In the same way as an adolescent encounters growing pains, so does a business as it reaches certain stages of its development.

These stages are critical and it is important to recognise them. Whilst they may be difficult to spot from within, an outside observer will more clearly see them and for this reason alone it is wise to counsel professional advice from time to time.

Initially a visit from your bank's Business Advisory Service or Corporate Division may prove to be the best investment you ever made; indeed, some visits are completely free of charge. Alternatively — or additionally — make use of a management consultancy firm. I.C.F.C., through its Consultants Ltd. subsidiary, offers such a service.

As a first step, however, make your own assessment of progress and the changing circumstances in which your business finds itself. Before you look any further, study your profit record.

Are You Doing As Well As You Could?

Many businessmen will tell you that they are making as much profit as it is possible to make in their particular line. Question them further and they are not even aware of the major controlling factors affecting profitability which are:

Selling more goods: The obvious one, although not necessarily the most productive in terms of net profit. Larger volume sales have to be financed and may also involve you in additional fixed costs, e.g. a factory extension or more delivery vehicles.

Increasing your selling prices: Perhaps the most difficult move to make in competitive markets but always one worth further investigation. Even a small uplift in prices can make a major difference to real profits.

Cutting costs: These may be prime costs, i.e. labour, materials and any other 'direct' expenditure, or overheads like the telephone bill or the postage account. Different suppliers might be found, items purchased in greater bulk with larger discounts, or simply more careful control maintained of expenses.

Changing the product mix: A technical expression meaning 'Sell more of the more profitable lines'. Ensure you know which are the greater money-spinners and direct your sales energies accordingly. Alternatively, seek more lucrative markets — such as overseas — for your products.

Before proceeding any further, therefore, make certain your firm is as efficient as it possibly can be in each of these areas.

It is interesting to see how, for instance, a 10% increase in sales compares with a 2% uplift in your selling prices:

		Original	Sell 10% more	Increase prices by 2%
Sales	£	10,000	11,000	10,200
Cost	£	8,000	8,800	8,000
Profit	£	2,000	2,200	2,200
Increase in profit			+10%	+10%

It is likely that the effort needed to sell 10% more goods (apart from any extra costs involved) could be far greater than implementing a 2% price rise, yet the net effect may be the same in each case.

Costs do not, of course, rise (or fall) quite like this, i.e. in equal proportions, but the example does help to highlight the situation. Remember also that higher prices may, at least temporarily, dampen demand.

Product mix, mentioned above, can also have some startling implications. One company making four different products turned over £240,000 in one year and showed a return of £45,000. The following year's sales were up to £270,000 and a profit in the region of £50,000 was hoped for.

When the accounts were audited, the directors were shocked to learn that the profit for the year was down to £26,500. Entirely behind this downturn was the different sales mix, where more of the less profitable products had been sold. From the actual results shown in the following table you can see how important it is for you to:

(a) know how much contribution to profit each product provides; and

STAND ON YOUR OWN TWO FEET WITH OUR SQUARE FEET.

English Estates have workshops available throughout England in both town and country. All designed and constructed to the highest of standards. All with very attractive rents. And we'll give you all the help and advice you need to ensure that getting started is as quick and easy as possible.

- Simple Easy In Easy Out 3 month tenancy agreements.
- No solicitor necessary.
- Building maintenance and insurance inclusive in the rent.

For more information and full details of workshops available close to you contact our nearest office.

ENGLISH ESTATES

More properties to get you going.
More help to get you growing.

ASHBOURNE (0335) 44616
BIRMINGHAM (021) 455 8828
CHATHAM (0634) 815081-6
CONSETT (0207) 590192
DONCASTER (0302) 66865
EXETER (0392) 211563/4
GATESHEAD (091) 487 4711
HARROGATE (0423) 523024

HEREFORD (0432) 54331
LIVERPOOL (051) 933 2020
NORWICH (0603) 617006
SLEAFORD (0529) 360219
THORNABY (0642) 765911
TRURO (0872) 40505
WORKINGTON (0946) 830469
YEOVIL (0935) 29601

(b) monitor sales product by product (preferably monthly) to give you a clear idea of progress throughout the accounting year.

		Year 1 £	Year 2 £
Product A		70,000	50,000
B		40,000	80,000
C		110,000	50,000
D		20,000	90,000
	Sales	240,000	270,000
Cost of sales: Product	A (40% of T/O)	28,000	20,000
	B (80% of T/O)	32,000	64,000
	C (50% of T/O)	55,000	25,000
	D (75% of T/O)	15,000	67,500
Total cost of sales		130,000	176,500
Gross profit		110,000	93,500
Overheads		65,000	67,000
Net pre-tax profit		45,000	26,500

Taking On A New Partner

One possible method of enabling you to expand is the acquisition of another partner or, in the case of a company, a co-director. Such a course is not usually without its problems.

The choice of the proper man, or woman, involves a certain amount of heart-searching.

What you will be getting — on paper at least, — is additional expertise, new contacts, a cash injection — or perhaps a blend of all three. But more significant, and what can be overlooked when negotiating the technical points, is the fact that you are accepting the possibility of working with this new face for the rest of your life.

Are your characteristics compatible? Do you honestly see yourself being able to harmoniously control the business in partnership with someone else?

If, after several days' deliberations, you satisfy yourself that it is going to work, however friendly the relationship draw up firm guidelines covering such topics as responsibility, authority and delegation. That way you will be providing for a pre-agreed 'judgement' should a dispute arise.

Agree the financial return well in advance. If shares are being purchased by your newcomer, what is the dividend policy to be? If a loan is being arranged, what is the rate of interest? And, just as important, how will the return of capital be treated?

Having agreed all these points in detail, it would be wise for your solicitor to draw up a contract. The small cost involved could pay dividends in the future.

Surprisingly, your 'new' partner could be the giant Shell company, Marks and Spencer's or G.E.C. These and other major companies have combined, with I.C.F.C. and the London Chamber of Commerce, to launch a series of incentives to help small concerns.

Various plans are on the drawing board, including the releasing of former petrol sites for industrial use and the seconding of Shell staff to assist with managerial functions for limited periods. Details may be obtained from Shell U.K.

Leasing

This alternative financing method becomes more readily available to the growing company than to the start-up concern. The main reason for this is that the leasing company will be interested in your Balance Sheet and annual accounts which, hopefully, will reveal a strengthening situation.

They will wish to safeguard, as far as possible, their future income — your leasing instalments — and since these may be spread over quite a number of years, a satisfactory and steady rate of return by your company should help to confirm your potential stability.

One major difference between leasing and hire purchase is the question of asset ownership. Whilst the user (the lessee) enjoys the benefits of use during the lifetime of the asset, it remains the property of the leasing company (the lessor).

Most capital goods can be leased, including:

Machinery of all kinds;
Computers;
Generators and compressors;
Motor vehicles, both commercial and personal (where there is also
    business use);
Office and hotel equipment;
Shopfittings (with certain exceptions);
Vending machines;
Professional apparatus, e.g. for doctors and dentists;
Agricultural and contractors' equipment;
Freight containers;
Ships, aircraft, etc

Apart from the ownership factor and the effect this can have on the company (discussed below), leasing tends to have more advantages than disadvantages, such as:

It avoids tying up large sums of cash;
It permits easier changes of assets for more updated ones;
It allows a 100% financing arrangement;
It provides long-term finance without diluting the control of
   ownership;
It assists with future budgeting of costs.

Leased items do not, of course, appear on your Balance Sheet and are not available as collateral for any other type of borrowing.

Leasing periods may vary according to the cost of the item involved but a 3 to 5 year range is the most common. Residual values can be agreed beforehand.

Discuss leasing with your financial advisor prior to any commitment; the Equipment Leasing Association will provide you with names of their members. Alternatively discuss the subject with your bank manager.

Factoring

A further financial resource which may become available to you as you expand is the factoring service offered by several leading specialists in this field. A minimum turnover of between £100,000 and £150,000 p.a. is expected, along with net assets of some £20,000 plus.

Basically, you 'sell' your outstanding debtors' claims to a factoring concern which agrees to advance up to 75/80% of monies owing to you.

Several combinations of services are offered, including the complete takeover of your sales ledger and the running of it on your behalf. One of the major advantages is usually a shorter average period outstanding of monies owed, with the resultant benefits passed to you. This is because factors are specialised in the handling of invoicing and subsequent chasing procedures.

The service isn't cheap but has to be compared with administration costs as well as the cost of borrowing working capital from your bank. Alternatively, you may have reached your borrowing limits on normal criteria, and factoring can provide an extra boost to cash flow.

There is a service charge of between 1% and 2½% of sales, plus an interest cost on sums paid to you in advance. The rate charged here is about the same margin over the Finance Houses Association base rate as you would be charged by your bank over their base rate.

Full protection against bad debts can be arranged and a confidential service is also available whereby your customers are not made aware of your use of a factor. Details from your bank or the Association of British Factors.

Extending or Moving

Either of these decisions rests on similar considerations and neither should be contemplated without a great deal of thought and proper research.

Many firms get carried away when an opportunity to relocate presents itself and failure to ask the right questions blinds the mind into accepting the move as a necessity. Just some of the important factors to be considered are:

(1) Why is extra space needed? Is our present capacity being fully and properly utilised?
(2) What are the precise costs of moving (or extending)? Are all mains services available? Has the land, or property, been professionally surveyed?
(3) Is repayment feasible over the period envisaged? Will it disrupt working capital needs?
(4) Is the cost justified in the light of projected increased profits?
(5) Will extra cash be needed for new plant and stock?
(6) Will deliveries (in or out) present a problem? Are raw materials as readily available?
(7) Is there an available labour source? Will transport present a problem?

If relocating, look at the various Government grants and loans available, some of which are explained in Chapter 9.

Factories may be cheaply offered in Development or Intermediate Areas through the Department of Industry in England, Scotland or Wales. Similar schemes exist in Northern Ireland and in Eire.

Timing your move is important to cause the minimum of disruption to production and, naturally, seasonal influences must be kept in mind.

Take full advantage of the move to look again at manufacturing, handling and storage methods. A golden opportunity exists at this time and, whilst it will undoubtedly create additional work at an abnormally busy time, its longer-term benefits will be felt later. Plan the move along these lines:

(1) Decide on future production strategies;
(2) Plan budgets for 2 or 3 years ahead and consider the resources needed to achieve these figures;
(3) Study existing methods of production, handling, storage and distribution with a view to improvements being made;
(4) Determine the correct sequence of the operation;
(5) Develop a block plan for the best possible work flow and break

this down into detailed charts decide on administrative and service areas,
(6) Purchase new plant and recruit labour as needed.

This may again be an opportune time to call in production experts such as I.C.F.C. or P.E.R.A. who will advise on the best plan of campaign. Specialist removal firms should be used where you are handling heavy or delicate machinery.

Remember, finally, that few moves go quite according to plan and be prepared for unexpected snags. Disruption cannot be avoided but its effects, with careful forethought, can be minimised. Explain to employees and customers what is happening, and keep a little extra cash on one side for, however thorough your estimates, the cost is bound to be somewhat higher!

Diversifying

Take stock of the environment from time to time and, if you envisage your markets diminishing, give some thought to the possibility of moving into a different line.

But beware of straying from your company's known strengths. Instead, make greater use of them in a different way.

Complete diversification can sometimes work, but many companies have learned to their cost the potential dangers of trying something entirely out of line with established products or markets. Stay within your capabilities.

Diversification works in several ways and may mean the creation of new products or services for marketing to your already established customers or, alternatively, developing new markets for a different product. Thirdly, new fields may open themselves to you through the acquisition of other concerns or the purchase of a manufacturing licence.

Take a close look at your resources — property, plant, labour and finance. Are they all being utilised to their most profitable extent? Analyse sales patterns and estimate demand, both in the short and long term. Research other possibilities.

It is as a result of such questioning, and a proper appraisal of the answers, that the need — if, indeed, there is one — for diversifying may become apparent.

The extent to which resources are to be committed, and the effect of this on current plans, obviously needs plenty of early thought and deliberation. Whilst all new business is a gamble, it would be foolish at this stage to jeopardise the business you have already worked hard to establish.

Beware of entering a high technology market when introducing a new product. It is safer to rely on more 'bread and butter' lines, unless you are fortunate enough in having such technical expertise 'in house' already. Again, aim at staying within the boundaries of the industry you know; let the big conglomerates of this world do the 'real' diversifying.

Mergers and Acquisitions

Meaning very much the same thing, although viewed differently depending on which side of the fence you are sitting, mergers can take place basically in any one of three ways:

(1) One company buying most or all of the shares in another;
(2) One company buying most or all of another's assets; or
(3) Two companies pooling their assets and liabilities in the formation of a new 'holding' company.

As we have seen above, diversification may be one object of a merger, but there are many others. For instance:

Eliminating some of the competition;
Gaining entry to new markets or buying up an already established product range;
Acquiring skills, e.g. managerial, technical, marketing, etc.,
Adding to production capacity;
Aiming at economies of scale.

The purchase price may consist of shares in the acquiring company, cash or a mixture of the two. Some complex bargaining situations open themselves up and financial advice at this stage, possibly from a merchant bank is the wisest course.

Although there may be little argument as to current values of the assets being bought (as opposed to their balance sheet values), it is in the grey area of future profitability, and therefore goodwill, that the two sides may find themselves in very differing camps.

No-one can accurately predict future performance and the issue becomes a bargaining one. Many smaller companies, when first approached, have an inflated opinion of their own worth and subsequent negotiations can become acrimonious.

Major acquisitions are tightly controlled by the City Code on Takeovers and Mergers on a non-statutory basis and legal advice, whether you are making an approach or being approached, is recommended.

Management Buy-Outs

Although the name is more recently coined, the phenomenon goes back many years. But during the early 1980's this type of company 'set-up' began to capture the imagination and success stories (along with a few failures) are now commonplace.

The recession was responsible for putting pressure upon large chunks of British industry to divest themselves of peripheral activities in order to streamline their operations, stem losses and provide a useful cash inflow. Incumbent managers seized upon the opportunity to secure their independence and to run the division for which they had always been responsible on lines more in keeping with a smaller company than as part of a giant combine.

Purchase prices vary according to the value of net assets being taken over as well as profit potential, but in most cases the stake provided by the new owners tends to be very small in relation to borrowed funds. Hence a 'high gearing' is created which in turn calls for adequacy of profits in order to pay interest. The business can thus be very vulnerable from Day 1 and is also occasionally saddled with inexperienced management.

It is a far different task to be master of a ship than head of a division, and all the necessary managerial skills do need to be in place to ensure success.

Many managers have, however, proved their capabilities and often get off to a good start by buying assets at a hefty discount, thus providing the margin demanded by financiers. Whilst some of the earlier management buy-outs looked relatively cheap, however, more latterly they are costing more and more, with assets sometimes going for a premium.

If you are involved with this type of purchase, contact one of the leading accountancy firms who employ specialists to guide you. The field is full of mines, and you must not attempt it alone. Your bank manager will put you in touch with the right advisers.

Acquiring a Computer

We have referred briefly to this in Chapter 4 but reiterate the essential preparations before you commit yourself here because so many businesses buy the wrong machinery to begin with. Apart from the cost involved, this can be a frustrating, time-wasting procedure, especially if all your data has to be reloaded a second time!

Success calls for careful planning and management commitment to the chosen system. The purpose of installing your computer must not be allowed to be overriden by the salesman's enthusiasm or the availability of additional 'gadgets'. Ask yourself initially 'Why do I need a computer system?' Good reasons may include:

(1) Improved clerical efficiency
(2) Improved cash flow as a result of speedier invoicing
(3) Better control of stocks
(4) Provision of topical management information
(5) Saving of additional staff

The best advice is to take advice. Seek out an *independent* computer consultant (many larger accountants will have one on their staff) and be prepared to pay his fee. It will save you a far greater sum in the long run.

Tell him precisely what your requirements are and he will find a compatible supplier. It is normally preferable to combine your hardware and software (programmes, etc.) needs in one source. That way, one supplier cannot blame the other if faults develop and vice versa.

You may prefer to widen your computer experience first by using a bureau. This will help to acclimatize you and your staff in computer 'jargon' and just what these machines can and cannot do for you.

Use of a bureau will save on capital costs and is a logical step towards acquiring your own system once familiarity has improved.

You can increase your computer knowledge by enrolling for a course on this topic. The Manpower Services Commission runs a grant scheme whereby up to £100 per week can be obtained in order to learn four main skills — programming, real-time programming, systems analysis and certain higher-level skills. Small businesses can also obtain grants towards the cost of evaluating how effective a computer system might be.

The Open University also provides completely impartial advice and demonstrations in the form of one-day seminars, aimed primarily at helping the smaller business to overcome the hurdle of introducing computers for the first time. Details available from the University.

Going Public

Perhaps this is every small businessman's dream, although some public company chairmen still rue the day they put their shares on the market and one, quite recently, has attempted to buy them back again!

Obviously we are now looking at well-established concerns where good growth and profit records will persuade a lot of people to part with their money in exchange for pieces of paper, i.e. share certificates.

Profits will need to have reached at least £250,000 in a full year and the cost of having your shares put on the Stock Exchange list will be at least this sum.

The first step will probably be a 'listing' on the U.S.M. (Unlisted Securities Market) or the Over The Counter market (O.T.C.). There are three major reasons why a company and its shareholders may find it advantageous to have shares in the company publicly traded:

(1) It enables present shareholders to realise part of the capital value of a successful business;
(2) It gives the company a wider market for the raising of equity or loan finance for development projects; and
(3) It can enhance the public image of the company and give it added status, factors which could contribute significantly to marketing the company's products.

Clearly, very serious thought has to be given to such a major move and competent advice — from your bank manager, accountant or solicitor should be sought. Merchant banks specialise in this sort of thing and the many implications — personal, financial and corporate — require thorough discussion with someone regularly dealing with new flotations.

Useful Addresses

Accepting Houses Committee
1 Crutched Friars
London EC3

Agricultural Credit Corporation
  Ltd.
Agriculture House
25/31 Knightsbridge
London SW1X 7NJ

Agricultural Mortgage Corporation
  Ltd.
Bucklesbury House
3 Queen Victoria Street
London EC4N 8OU

The Alliance of Small Firms and Self
  Employed People Ltd.
42 Vine Road
East Molesey
Surrey KT8 9LF

The Association of Certified and
  Corporate Accountants
22 Bedford Square
London WC1B 3HS

The Association of British
  Chambers of Commerce
Sovereign House
212a Shaftesbury Avenue
London WC2H 8EW

Association of British Factors
Markby's
Moor House
London Wall
London EC2Y 5HE

Association of Independent
  Businesses
Trowbray House
108 Weston Street
London SE1 3QB

British Overseas Trade Board
Export House
Ludgate Hill
London EC4M 7HU

British Standards Institution
2 Park Street
London W1A 2BS

British Export Houses Association
69 Cannon Street
London EC4N 5AB

British Franchise Association
75a Bell Street
Henley-on-Thames
Oxon RG9 2BD

British Steel Corporation (Industry)
  Ltd.
PO Box 403
33 Grosvenor Place
London SW1X 7JG

British Institute of Management
Management House
Parker Street
London WC2B 5CT

British Tourist Authority
Queen's House
64 St. James's Street
London SW1A 1NF

Business Education Council
76 Portland Place
London W1

Business in the Community
227A City Road
London EC1

Central Office of Information
Great George Street
London SW1P 3AQ

Charterhouse Development Ltd.
1 Paternoster Row
St. Paul's
London EC4P 4HP

Colt International Ltd.
Havant
Hants, PO9 2LY

Companies Registration Office
Companies House
Crown Way
Maindy
Cardiff

Confederation of British Industry
Centre Point
103 New Oxford Street
London WC1A 1DU

CBI Special Programmes Unit
58 St. James's Street
London SW1A 1LD

Co-operative Advisory Group
272-276 Pentonville Road
London N1 9JY

Council for Small Industries in
  Rural Areas
141 Castle Street
Salisbury
Wilts SP1 3TP

D.A.S. Legal Insurance
Dulverton House
Redcliffe Hill
Bristol

Deloitte, Haskins & Sells
PO Box 142
25 Bread Street
London EC4V 4AJ

Department of Employment
32 St. James's Square
London SW1 4JB

Department of Energy
Thames House South
Millbank
London SW1P 4QJ

Department of Industry
Millbank Tower
Millbank
London SW1P 4QU
(and local offices)

Department of Industry (Small
  Firms Division)
Abell House
John Islip Street
London SW1P 4LN

Department of Trade (Export
  Services)
1 Victoria Street
London SW1H 0ET

Design Council
28 Haymarket
London SW1Y 4SU

Dun & Bradstreet Ltd.
26/32 Clifton Street
London EC2P 2LY

Electrical Research Association
Cleeve Road
Leatherhead
Surrey KT22 7SA

Employers' Protection Insurance
    Services Ltd.
30 High Street
Sutton
Surrey

Engineering Council
Canberra House
Maltravers Street
London WC2R 3ER

Engineering Industries Association
Engineering House
Lyon Road
Harrow
Middlesex

English Tourist Board
(contact your local
Regional Office)

Equal Opportunities Commission
Overseas House
Quay Street
Manchester M3 3HN

Equipment Leasing Association
14 Queen Anne's Gate
London SW1

Estate Duties Investment Trust Ltd.
    (EDITH)
91 Waterloo Road
London SE1 8XP

European Investment Bank
c/o I.C.F.C.
Piercy House
7 Copthall Avenue
London EC2R 7DD

Export Credit Guarantee
    Department (E.C.G.D.)
Aldermanbury House
London EC2P 2EL

Extel Statistical Services Ltd.
1 East Harding Street
London EC4P 4HB

FMC (Meat) Ltd.
19-23 Knightsbridge
London SW1 7NF

The Forum of Private Business
Ruskin Rooms
Drury Lane
Knutsford
Cheshire WA16 0ED

Franchise Advisory Centre Ltd.
32 Stockwell Park Crescent
London SW9

Furniture Industry Research
    Association
Maxwell Road
Stevenage
Herts. SG1 2EW

Government Statistical Service
Great George Street
London SW1P 3AQ
Group 4 Total Security Ltd.

Farncombe House
Broadway
Worcs. WR12 7LJ

H.M.S.O.
Atlantic House
Holborn Viaduct
London EC1P 1BN

Highlands and Islands
    Development Board
Bridge House
Bank Street
Inverness IV1 1QR

Hotel & Catering Industry Training
    Board
PO Box 18
Ramsey House
Central Square
Wembley
Middlesex

I.I.I.
91 Waterloo Road
London SE1 8XP
(and local offices)

I.C.F.C. (Training and
  Management Consultants Ltd.)
5 Victoria Street
Windsor
Berks S14 1EZ

Industrial Development Authority
  of Ireland
100 Belfast Road
Holywood
Co. Down BT1 9QX

Institute of Directors
116 Pall Mall
London SW1Y 5ED

Institute of Marketing
Marketing House
Cooksham
Berkshire

Institute of Practitioners in
  Advertising
44 Belgrave Square
London SW1X 8QS

Institute of Chartered Accountants
Moorgate Place
London EC2P 2BJ

Institute of Chartered Patent
  Agents
Staple Inn Buildings
London WC1

Institute of Export
World Trade Centre
St. Katherine's Way,
London E1 9AA

Institute of Freight Forwarders
Suffield House
9 Paradise Road
Richmond
Surrey TW9 1SA

Institute of Management
  Consultants
23-24 Cromwell Place
London SW7 2LG

Institute of Small Businesses
1 Whitehall Place
London SW1A 2HD

IREX
Snow House
123 Southwark Street
London SE1 0JF

Kalamazoo Ltd.
Northfield
Birmingham B31 2RW

Land Settlement Association Ltd.
43 Cromwell Road
London SW7

Lands Improvement Co. Ltd.
63 Piccadilly
London W1

Law Society
113 Chancery Lane
London WC2A 1PL

Local Eyes
111 Wood Lane
Sutton Coldfield
West Midlands

Location of Offices Bureau (LoB)
Longsdale Chambers
27 Chancery Lane
London WC2A 1NN

London Enterprise Agency
  (LENTA)
69 Cannon Street
London EC4N 5AB

Machine Tool Industry Research
  Association
Hulley Road
Hurdsfield
Macclesfield
Cheshire SK10 2NE

Maclaren Publishers Ltd.
PO Box 109
Davis House
69/77 High Street
Croydon CR9 1QH

Manpower Services Commission
Selkirk House
166 High Holborn
London WC1V 6PF

Market Research Society
51 Charles Street
London W1X 7PA

National Association of Shop-
    keepers
Lynch House
91 Mansfield Road
Nottingham NG1 3FN

The National Chamber of Trade
Enterprise House
Henley-on-Thames
Oxon RG9 ITU

National Federation of the Self-
    Employed and Small Businesses
32 St. Anne's Road West
Lytham St. Annes
Lancashire FY8 1NY

National Engineering
Laboratory
East Kilbride
Glasgow G75 0QU

National Physical Laboratory
Teddington
Middlesex TW11 0LW

National Research Development
    Corporation (NRDC)
Kingsgate House
66 Victoria Street
London SW1E 9SL

National Enterprise Board (NEB)
12-18 Grosvenor Gardens
London SW1W 0DS

National Freight Corporation
Argosy House
215 Great Portland Street
London W1

National Allied Societies
Enterprise House
Henley-on-Thames
Oxon. RG9 1TU

Northern Ireland Development
    Agency
11 Berkeley Street
London W1

Office of Fair Trading
Bromyard Avenue
Acton
London W3 7BB

Open University
    Associate Students
Central Office
PO Box 76
Milton Keynes
MK3 5HW

Patent Office
25 Southampton Buildings
Chancery Lane
London WC2A 1AW

Portakabin Ltd.
Huntington
York YO3 9PT

Production Engineering
    Research Association (PERA)
Melton Mowbray
Leicestershire LE13 0PB

Registry of Business Names
Pembroke House
40-56 City Road
London EC1Y 1BB

Royal Institute of British Architects
66 Portland Place
London W1N 4AB

Scottish Business in the
  Community
Eagle Star House
25 St Andrews Square
Edinburgh EH2 1AF

Scottish Development Agency
162 Telford Road
Edinburgh
Shell U.K. Ltd.
PO Box 148

Shell-Mex Ltd.
Strand
London WC2

Small Firms Information Service
(See Department of Industry/Small
  Firms Division) (and local
  offices)

Small Business Capital Fund
88 Baker Street
London W1M 1DC

Small Business Bureau
32 Smith Square
Westminster
London SW1 3HH

Small Industries Council for Rural
  Areas in Scotland
27 Walker Street
Edinburgh EH3 7HZ

Trade Indemnity Credit Insurance
12-34 Great Eastern Street
London EC2A 3AX

Union of Independent Companies
71 Fleet Street
London EC4

Venture Capital Report
2 The Mall
Bristol BS8 4DR

Welsh Development Agency
Treforest Industrial Estate
Pontypridd
Mid Glamorgan CF37 5UT

Welsh Tourist Agency
Dept. R.8
PO Box 151
Cardiff CF1 2XN

Present Value of £1
(All figures are after the decimal point)

YEARS

%	1	2	3	4	5	6	7	8	9	10	11	12	13	14	15
1	9901	9803	9706	9610	9515	9420	9327	9235	9143	9053	8963	8874	8787	8700	8613
2	9804	9612	9423	9238	9057	8880	8706	8535	8368	8203	8043	7885	7730	7579	7430
3	9709	9426	9151	8885	8626	8375	8131	7894	7664	7441	7224	7014	6810	6611	6419
4	9615	9246	8890	8548	8219	7903	7599	7307	7026	6756	6496	6246	6006	5775	5553
5	9524	9070	8638	8227	7835	7462	7107	6768	6446	6139	5847	5568	5303	5051	4810
6	9434	8900	8396	7921	7473	7050	6651	6274	5919	5584	5268	4970	4688	4423	4173
7	9346	8734	8163	7629	7130	6663	6227	5823	5439	5083	4751	4440	4150	3878	3624
8	9259	8573	7938	7350	6806	6302	5835	5403	5002	4632	4289	3971	3677	3405	3152
9	9174	8417	7722	7084	6499	5963	5470	5019	4604	4224	3875	3555	3262	2992	2745
10	9091	8264	7513	6830	6209	5645	5132	4665	4241	3855	3505	3186	2897	2633	2394
11	9009	8116	7312	6587	5935	5346	4817	4339	3909	3522	3173	2858	2575	2320	2090
12	8929	7972	7118	6355	5674	5066	4523	4039	3606	3220	2875	2567	2292	2046	1827
13	8850	7831	6931	6133	5428	4803	4251	3762	3329	2946	2607	2307	2042	1807	1599
14	8772	7695	6750	5921	5194	4556	3996	3506	3075	2697	2366	2076	1821	1597	1401
15	8695	7561	6575	5718	4971	4323	3759	3269	2843	2472	2149	1869	1625	1413	1229
16	8621	7432	6407	5523	4761	4104	3538	3050	2630	2267	1954	1685	1452	1252	1079
17	8547	7305	6244	5337	4561	3898	3332	2848	2434	2080	1778	1520	1299	1110	0949
18	8475	7182	6086	5158	4371	3704	3139	2660	2255	1911	1619	1372	1163	0985	0835
19	8403	7062	5934	4987	4190	3521	2959	2457	2090	1756	1476	1240	1040	0876	0736
20	8333	6944	5787	4823	4019	3349	2791	2326	1938	1615	1346	1122	0935	0779	0649
21	8264	6830	5645	4665	3855	3186	2633	2176	1799	1486	1228	1015	0839	0693	0573
22	8197	6719	5507	4514	3700	3033	2486	2038	1670	1369	1122	0920	0754	0618	0507
23	8130	6610	5374	4369	3552	2888	2348	1909	1552	1262	1026	0834	0678	0551	0448
24	8065	6504	5245	4230	3411	2751	2218	1789	1443	1164	0938	0757	0610	0492	0397
25	8000	6400	5120	4096	3277	2621	2097	1678	1342	1074	0859	0687	0550	0440	0352

Index

Accidents 63, 77
Accountant 64, 70–72, 146
Accounting methods 64–65
Accounting rate of return method
    (A.R.R.) 107
Acquisitions 143
Advertising 85–86
Advice 10–11
After-sales service 19–20
Agricultural Mortgage Corporation 30,
    117
Annual Accounts 50–51
Architect 59
Asset records 42
Auditor 50

Balance sheets 36, 50, 51, 104
Bank manager 11, 34, 36, 71, 146
Bankruptcy 69, 121
Bill of Exchange 96, 97
Borrowing 28, 29
Break-even charts 44
British Overseas Trade Board (B.O.T.B.)
    91
British Steel Corporation 119
British Technology Group 116
Budgets 43, 103–4
Business counsellors 21
Business Expansion Scheme 34
Business in the Community (B.I.C.) 23
Business Monitors 21–22
Business plan 120
Buying an established business 65–66

Capital costs 17, 25
Capital expenditure 31
Capital gearing 121
Capital projects 106–9

Capital risks 13
Cash book 40–41
Cash flow 18, 140
Cash projection 34, 36–38
Chambers of Trade and Commerce 12
Clearing banks 29, 117
Collateral. See Security
Communications 59–60
Company growth 135–46
Competition 15–16
Computers 65, 144–45
Confidence 6
Consulting Services Information Bureau
    21
Consumer behaviour 82
Contracts 106, 139
Corporation tax 47, 48
Cost centres 105
Cost considerations 16–17
Cost cutting 136
Cost sources 105
Costing
    marginal 38, 105
    product 38–40
    projects 25–28, 106–9
    putting to use 105–6
Council for Small Industries in Rural
    Areas (CoSIRA) 30
Courses 7, 8, 95
Credit control 42
Credit-rating agencies 23

Debenture 35, 115
Decisionmaking 5
Demand elasticity 17
Depreciation 17
Design Centre 84
Determination 9
Development bodies 31

Direct costs 39, 105
Directories 22
Discipline 130
Discounted cash flow (DCF) 108–9
Discounts 43
Distribution network 83–84
Diversification 10, 18, 142
Documentary letter of credit 96
Documentation 95

80/20 rule 81, 111
Employee welfare 128–30
English Industrial Estates Corporation 56
Enterprise Agencies 23
Enterprise Allowance Scheme 8
Enterprise Zones 54–55
Enthusiasm 9
Environment study 14–15
Estate Duties Investment Trust (EDITH) 116–17
European Community 119
European Investment Bank 119
Expansion 135–46
Expertise 7–8
Export Credits Guarantee Department (E.C.G.D.) 97–98
Export payments 96
Exporting 90–99
External factors 18, 100

Factoring 140
Factory worker versus shopkeeper 3–4
Family aspects 6
Finance companies 29
Finance sources 25–33, 114–22, 140
Financial advantages 2–3
Financial planning 63
Fixtures and fittings 25–26
Flexibility 9–10
Franchise operations 67
Freeports 99
Fringe benefits 130

Goodwill 19, 20, 66
Government controls 18
Government grants 31–33, 54, 61, 63, 117–19, 141
Government Statistical Service 22
Guarantee terms 20

Health and Safety at Work etc., Act 63, 76
Health demands 6
Highlands and Islands Development Board 31
Hire purchase 29, 61, 139
Holiday priorities 129
Home-based businesses 54
Humanity 10

Indirect costs 39, 105
Industrial and Commercial Finance Corporation (I.C.F.C.) 30, 38, 116
Industrial buildings 48
Industrial Development Certificate 58
Information requirements 20
Information services 22, 74
Information sources 12, 19, 20–24, 93
Insurance 76–78, 98
Insurance broker 72
Insurance companies 30
Integrity 10
Interviewing 62
Investment trusts 117
Investors in Industry 30

Job description 124, 125–26
Job efficiency 132–34
Job rotation 129
Judgement 9

Key employees 130

Labour aspects 18
Labour bill 17
Labour force 61–63, 123–24
Lead time 110
Leadership 5
Leasing 30, 61, 139–40
Legal costs 74
Legislation 18, 63, 73–76, 100, 127
Lending values 35–36
Letterheads 71
Libraries 12, 21, 93
Licensing 19
Life cycle 81
Life policy 28, 77
Limited companies 35, 47, 49, 66, 69–71
Liquidity ratios 46–47
Listed companies 146
Loans 29, 33, 121, 141

Location of Offices Bureau 58
London Enterprise Agency 57
Losses 13, 47, 70

Management accounts 103–4
Management buy-outs 144
Management Extension Programme 8
Management structure 124
Manpower planning 124, 125
Manpower requirements 124
Manpower Services Commission 7, 8, 145
Marginal costing 38, 105
Margins 81
Market investigation 14–24
Market research 90–93
Market Research Society 21
Marketing 79–88
Material costs 17
Merchant banks 30, 115–17, 146
Mergers 143
Money aspects 2–3, 12–13
    see also Finance
Mortgage 57, 58, 115

National Federation of Self-Employed
        and Small Businesses 57, 73
National Insurance 42, 49
National Union of Small Shopkeepers of
        Great Britain and Northern Ireland
        11
Net present value (N.P.V.) 108–9

Oakwood Loan Finance 116
Objectives 79–80, 102, 126–27
Open account 96–97
Open University 145
Organisation and Method Study 134
Overdraft 29
Overheads 17, 66, 105
Overtrading 121

Packaging 86–87
Pareto's Law 81, 111
Partnerships 69, 70, 138–39
Patents 48, 73
Payback method 108
PAYE 42, 49, 65
Pensions 2, 77
Performance ratios 45–46
Personnel 61–63, 66

Personnel management 123–24
Petrol companies 31
Petty cash 42
Planning permission 18
Plant and machinery 25–26, 48, 60–61
Portakabin 59
Post Office 60, 117
Practicability 9
Premises 54–59
Present situation evaluation 1–2
Price fluctuations 64
Price guides 38
Price increases 17
Price tickets 86
Pricing policies 80–82
Printing 87
Product development 82–83
Product mix 136
Professional advice 68–78
Profit 28, 79, 80, 106
Profit and loss account 36, 38, 50, 52, 104
Profit levels 121
Profit margins 29
Profit records 135–38, 145
Profitability 121, 135
Promotion 84–85, 93–95
Public company 145–46
Purchases ledger 42

Quality Circles 133

Ratios 45–47
Records 40–42, 64, 65, 124
Regulations 87
Relocation 141–42
Research and development 17, 112–13
Research needs 10–11
Retirement 77
Return on capital 45
Risk factors 6, 19, 29

Salary levels 127
Sale and leaseback 115
Sales force 88–89
Sales ledger 42
Sales monitoring 138
Savings scheme 129
Science Parks 56
Seasonal influences 17–18, 64
Security 1, 6, 35, 59
Self-analysis 5

Selling 88–89
Shopkeeper versus factory worker 3–4
Simon's Law 100
Small Company Innovation Fund 116
Small Firms Information Service 12, 21
Small Industries Council for Rural Areas
   31
Social events 129
Sole trader 68
Solicitor 20, 43, 66, 70, 72, 73, 139, 146
Sources and Uses of Funds statement 51
Staff induction 128
Staff promotions 130
Staff records 124
Staff recruiting 62, 123
Staff report form 128
Staff suggestions 130
Staff training. See Training
Starting procedure 1–13
Statutes 74–76
Statutory rights 2
Stickability 6
Stock and stock control 49, 63–64, 110–11
Stock valuations 111–12
Strategic planning 100–13
Strikes 127

Targets 126
Taxation 47–49, 70
Technological advances 15, 112
Temperament 5
Terms of payment 42
Test marketing 87–88
Trade Associations 21
Trade Indemnity Credit Insurance 43
Trade journals 19
Trade union 2, 62
Training 7, 62–63, 130–32
Transport 59

Under-capitalisation 121

Variances 39
VAT 42, 49, 65
Vehicles 48, 60
Venture capital 23, 116

Wife's salary 13
Willpower 6
Work-in-progress 49
Work study 133
Worker-directors 129
Working capital 26
Working conditions 128